Remnants of Hegel

SUNY series in Contemporary Continental Philosophy

Dennis J. Schmidt, editor

Remnants of Hegel

Remains of Ontology, Religion, and Community

Félix Duque

Translated by
Nicholas Walker

Published by State University of New York Press, Albany

© 2018 State University of New York

All rights reserved

No part of this book may be used or reproduced in any manner whatsoever without written permission. No part of this book may be stored in a retrieval system or transmitted in any form or by any means including electronic, electrostatic, magnetic tape, mechanical, photocopying, recording, or otherwise without the prior permission in writing of the publisher.

For information, contact State University of New York Press, Albany, NY
www.sunypress.edu

Library of Congress Cataloging-in-Publication Data

Names: Duque, Félix, author. | Walker, Nicholas, 1954– translator.
Title: Remnants of Hegel : remains of ontology, religion, and community / Félix Duque ; translated by Nicholas Walker.
Other titles: Hegel. English
Description: Albany : State University of New York Press, [2018] | Series: SUNY series in contemporary continental philosophy | First publication of work—original language not published.| Includes bibliographical references and index.
Identifiers: LCCN 2017056057 | ISBN 9781438471570 (hardcover : alk. paper) | ISBN 9781438471587 (pbk. : alk. paper) | ISBN 9781438471594 (ebook)
Subjects: LCSH: Hegel, Georg Wilhelm Friedrich, 1770–1831.
Classification: LCC B2948 .D82613 2018 | DDC 193—dc23
LC record available at https://lccn.loc.gov/2017056057

10 9 8 7 6 5 4 3 2 1

Contents

Preface   vii

Acknowledgments   xiii

Chapter I. Substrate and Subject (Hegel in the
Aftermath of Aristotle)   1
   1. Aristotle: A Certain Underlying Nature and the
      Individual "Thing"   1
   2. Not Substance, But Just as Much Subject   13
   3. The Reflexive Movement of Thinking   21
   4. The Unveiling of Substance as the Genesis of
      the Concept   23
   5. Begging the Question of Beginning   25

Chapter II. Hegel on the Death of Christ
(*Ich bin der Kampf selbst*)   29
   1. The Infinite Value of Subjectivity   29
   2. The Death of Christ and the Commencement
      of History   34
   3. The Strange Heart of Reason   39
   4. "I Am the Unity of Fire and Water"   43
   5. Natural Death and the Death of Death   47

Chapter III. Death Is a Gulp of Water
(*La Terreur* in World History)   55
   1. Hegel and the Revolution—After Marxism   55
   2. Living and Thinking One's Own Time   58

3. A Literal Reading of Hegel 61
4. Hegel's Two "Terrors" 64
5. Metal and Water: Beheading and Drowning 74
6. Fanaticism as a Chemical Precipitate 78
7. An Inverted Allegory of the Cave 83
8. From Absolute Negativity to the Element of Freedom 87

Chapter IV. Person, Freedom, and Community 93
1. The Entire Remnant of the Idea 93
2. Person as a Relational Nature 98
3. Abstract Right and Legal Recognition 102
4. Ethical Life and Bourgeois Virtues 107
5. A Strange Sort of Redemption 111

Chapter V. The Errancy of Reason (The Perishing of the Community) 115
1. The Devil, the Good Lord, and Human Blood 115
2. Man as the Possibility of God: *Passio Christi* 119
3. Cultus and Eucharist as *Manducatio Spiritualis* 125
4. The Spirit as the Wound of Time 128
5. The Fullness of Time as the Exhaustion of Time 133

Notes 135

Index 157

Preface

From the beginning, Aristotle takes *prima philosophia* to be the knowledge that we ultimately seek.[1] We should likewise remember that Aristotle's *Physics*—as an ancient title of this work, *Phusikē Akroasis*, already attests—employs an acroamatic method, namely one that is specifically addressed to hearers and listeners in a context of free dialogue and public discourse (something that Kant also desired and expected in response to his own critical philosophy), a method that was unfolded in and through the continual *confrontation*, *refutation*, and *refinement* of conflicting theses. This procedure reveals a certain affinity to that interplay of *question and answer* that Gadamer has proposed in our own times as the hermeneutic approach par excellence.

If something of the kind is already at work in "the master of those that know," the founder of *prima philosophia*, this is even clearer in the case of Kant, the founder of the *metaphysics of experience*, who proceeds through *discursive demonstrations* that are developed in the context of a language that is actually never simply static or fixed in character. As Kant explicitly says in the "Discipline of Pure Reason" in the first *Critique*, philosophy is restricted to the *analysis* of concepts, which is why its judgments (i.e., the *principles* of the corresponding Analytic) can be demonstrated "only indirectly through the relation of these concepts to something altogether contingent, namely *possible experience*."[2] Even if this is so, from a cautious Kantian perspective, it must also be recognized that whereas possible experience is, in any particular case, something contingent, the *possibility of experience* as such is absolutely not contingent, for it ultimately depends on an absolute presupposition. Or to put this in another way, it depends on the hypothesis of the *Absolute*. However, it is evident that the Absolute as such cannot be demonstrated. As we can see from the three *Critiques*, it is something that can only be *postulated*, precisely for the sake of that knowledge or science (*epistēmē*) that was always sought but never attained.

As is widely recognized, this was the challenge with which German Idealism generally, and Hegel's thought in particular, found itself compelled to confront. Thus, the question for us is whether it is legitimate to apply the term "hermeneutics," understood in the broadest sense, to Hegel's celebrated dialectical method, especially as presented in the *Phenomenology of Spirit* and the *Science of Logic*. Now it could be said that the path pursued by Hegel does not offer a new way of knowing at all. What it does instead is to interpret, reconstruct, and refine the "first order" bodies of knowledge (of mathematics, the natural sciences, the sociopolitical and cultural sciences) to arrive, on the one hand, at a complex awareness of the Absolute as a *singulare tantum* (as *ab-solutes Wissen*) where certainty and truth, *theoria* and *praxis*, the I and the world, come to coincide, and on the other, to articulate a kind of universal grammar of being, ultimately comprehended in terms of the Idea.

This can properly be understood as a procedure *in actu exercito*, as the practice of a specific Hegelian "hermeneutics" that consists in a relentless but internal "destruction" or dismantling not only in relation to the particular opinions and perspectives of individuals and entire epochs regarding the Absolute, but also and especially in relation to all possible definitions of the Absolute, subjecting each and every particular logical determination to critique and sublation (*Aufhebung*) as they are methodically presented and just as methodically refuted throughout the entire *Science of Logic* (for Kant was right, after all, about the impossibility of *demonstrating* the Absolute). Indeed "the beginning of the end" of Hegel's *Logic*, namely the beginning of the chapter on the *absolute Idea*, allows us to glimpse that what really constitutes the work itself is not so much its supposed refutation of every attempt to define the Absolute as the internal and *essential* contradiction between the explicit claim of the *Logic* (where we are told that the Idea is true being itself and the truth of being, is truth in its entirety and the only truth) and the very condition that permits this goal to be achieved in the first place. (Hegel himself writes: "All the rest is error, confusion, opinion, striving, arbitrariness, and transience.") Yet all of that "rest," all of what "remains," is just the whole of the *Logic* itself. The truth is that the complete self-suppression of every synthesis of logical determinations that aspires to express the Absolute once and for all is also precisely what signifies the human way of approaching the Absolute *a contrario sensu*.

If this is the case, then Hegel's hermeneutic metaphysics is nothing but the strenuous labor of rationally reconstructing the matter (*die Sache*) of thinking itself. Yet what, precisely, is being reconstructed here? In fact, in the preface to the second edition of the *Science of Logic* Hegel recognizes the existence of an *instinctive* and *unconscious* logic whose forms and determinations "always remain imperceptible and incapable of becoming objective even as they emerge in language" (this is a strange logic that, contrary to Hegel's explicit intentions, we can never fully know, one that eludes the kind of being that properly belongs to the *logos*, in short, an *illogical* logic). The entire *Logic* is nothing but a relentless attempt to furnish a *conscious and deliberate reconstruction* of fugitive and fleeting linguistic forms and determinations. And yet Hegel's argument is not mystical or romantic in any sense. It is precisely a closure or completion of thinking (an *Abgeschlossenheit des Denkens*) that implicitly invokes what has been banished from the process of closure itself. It is no accident therefore that in the transition from the *Science of Logic* to the *Philosophy of Nature*, in the "quantum leap" of the Idea as and toward nature, that this latter should appear as *Abfall*, as waste, as a falling away or remnant of the Idea, or rather, even as the Idea's act of self-refusal. Yet if this is so, how can spirit ever heal itself from this falling away? For if nature—as Hegel says—expresses "the impotence of the Concept" (i.e., if it is impotent over against the Concept), will not the Concept itself perhaps reveal its impotence too, not only with regard to the meaningless profusion of the natural (the *luxus naturae* that was so discussed during the age of the Baroque), but also with regard to the Concept's own capacity to master, *without remainder*, the very determinations which constitute it?

If all this is so, then it must unfortunately be recognized that the wounds of the Spirit do not necessarily heal without leaving any scars. The Hegelian system, impressive as it is, ultimately reveals itself as a miscarried attempt to reconcile nature and *theoria*, individuality and collective *praxis*.

The aim of this book, therefore, is to support this claim by exploring Hegel's philosophy in terms of the following five steps:

1. The conversion of metaphysics into the logic of a subject that is never capable of mastering itself as substance.

2. The effects of this unfulfilled attempt in the tragic interpretation of the death of Christ as at once the Subject par excellence and the Man of Sorrows.

3. The possibility of mitigating or evading this consequence through Revolution: through the triumph of absolute freedom (and thus the liberation from Nature and God).

4. The interiorization of freedom in morality, and the transformation of the idea of the "person" as an abstract ground of the "Constitutional State" based on "man" tout court, or *Homo oeconomicus*: the divided subject (*bourgeois-citoyen*) of the emerging industrial and market-governed society.

5. The examination, in the final chapter, of the dialectical-speculative "translation," in the light of the anachronistic conception of "community," of the current failure of the system that attempts to assume and control the contradictions of the modern nation-state and the international system of industrial capitalism.

Remnants of Hegel is not, and is not intended to be, merely a book about Hegel. It is intended to be a book about the wounds that, perhaps in contrast to the deliberate intentions of the great melancholic Swabian philosopher, can be exposed in texts that may still provoke new thinking with regard to other remnants, in other words, to what remains of that which once proudly called itself the West, even if probably thereby neglected the ultimate meaning of the word *Abendland*, the Land of the Setting Sun. Perhaps we are beginning to understand the reason for such a dark name.

Acknowledgments

The core of this book dates back to an occasion in August 2016, when I was invited by the International Summer School of Ontology (ISSO, now called ISP: International School of Philosophy, Grado, Italy) to give three seminars on Hegel, which after being modified and expanded now correspond to chapters I, II and IV. I would like to express my gratitude to Valerio Rocco, a colleague and friend from the Universidad Autónoma of Madrid, who carefully read the texts in question, made important suggestions, participated actively in the seminars, and subsequently encouraged me in the process of publication with great care and perseverance. Chapters III and V are revised versions of a lecture I gave at the Universidad Complutense of Madrid and of a course on Hegel's *Philosophy of Religion* that I taught at the University of Buenos Aires. The structure and purpose of the book was conceived in the second semester of the academic year 2013/2014, during an undergraduate course at the Universidad Autónoma, specifically devoted to the "Introduction" and the "Preliminary Concept" of Hegel's *Encyclopedia of the Philosophical Sciences*. I am grateful to Eduardo Zazo for his collaboration and active participation in this course. I owe important suggestions (both on the concept of "revolution" and on Adorno's interpretation of Hegelian philosophy) to Marcela Vélez, who is finishing her PhD dissertation on the topic "Adorno and the Revolution." I would like to thank Sergio Montecinos (Berlin/Santiago de Chile) for being an excellent discussant on Hegel's logic and metaphysics, especially regarding the "logic of reflection." Leonardo Mattana is currently writing a dissertation on the transformation of Kant's *antinomies* in the context of Hegel's *Logic* and has contributed significantly to the development of my own research with his insightful questions and comments.

Andrew Buchwalter (University of North Florida) deserves a special mention for the faith he showed with regard to the manuscript, and for his discussions with me regarding different ethical and political aspects of Hegel's philosophy. In addition, I am honored here to acknowledge my friendship with Vincenzo Vitiello (Salerno/Milan), with whom I have worked on many shared interests and problems for more than thirty years. I still continue to learn every day from his astonishing knowledge, especially in relation to religious questions, as indeed I have also done from Bruno Forte, archbishop of Chieti-Vasto, Italy. Lastly, of course, I am very happy to express my debt to the translator: Nicholas Walker (Cambridge), whose work is beyond all praise. Our continuous fruitful communication and his exceptional philosophical knowledge have considerably improved the quality of the manuscript. I have also enjoyed our exchange of views on many other matters of literary, artistic, and musical interest (especially our discussions regarding Bach, Händel, and Cristóbal Halffter).

I extend my gratitude and my friendship to them all.

Tres Cantos (Madrid), August 2017

Chapter I

Substrate and Subject
(Hegel in the Aftermath of Aristotle)

1. Aristotle: A Certain Underlying Nature and the Individual "Thing"

One does not need be a *militant* Heideggerian to recognize that "metaphysics," from its very beginning, has posed a problem that is by no means easy to resolve, and, what is more, that metaphysics has thereby posed itself as a problem too. Metaphysics is precisely *this* problem: that of providing an investigation (*skepsis*) into the relation between permanence and change, between being and becoming. Naturally we cannot resolve this question by eliminating one of the two contrasted terms, at least not without falling either into a hyper-Parmenidean position like that defended by Zeno of Elea or into the kind of corrosive relativism espoused by Gorgias or Cratylus. That the relation would have to bestow preeminence on that which is (*to on*) over against "things which come to be" (*ta gignomena*) has been inscribed in the very terminology of the philosophical tradition ever since the verb *keimai* ("to lie") was specifically chosen to express the primacy of *constant presence*, of that which continues to be the same as itself, that which endures and thereby merits confidence in its reliability. And this is the source of the two compound expressions, the *hypokeimenon* and the *antikeimenon*—namely "that which lies beneath as ground or foundation," on the one hand, and "that which lies before or over against us," on the other (in the masculine gender *ho antikeimenos* means the "adversary" or "opponent," and thus in the religious context also the Devil).

And the task that falls to metaphysics is to transform this opposition of something considered in terms of stability (as *hypostasis*) and something else that resists or hinders it (as *antistasis*) into a relation of subordination on the part of the latter (that which is "opposed") with regard to the former (that which "underlies"), or to put this in another way: into the *dominion* of the former over the latter. Moreover, and quite independently of the *vexata quaestio* of whether the ancient Greeks did or did not accord a certain primacy to the reality of "things" with respect to the one who contemplates or beholds this reality (namely to the human being), the various uses of the expression *hypokeimenos* make it possible for us (namely *we ourselves* as human beings of late modernity) to understand very clearly what or rather *who* it is that truly stands at the ground or foundation, who it is that acts from "below," transforming obstacles and hindrances into so many stimuli and opportunities for its own activity. Thus *ho hypokeimenos chronos*, for example, is "the actual present time, the time that lies within our hands." And *ta hypokeimena* are "the things which lie within our power." And, finally, *to hypokeimenon* also signifies, according to a classic French lexicon of the Greek language, "le sujet proposé, le texte."[1] It is of course well known that in various European languages the words *le sujet*, *the subject*, *il soggetto*, (a film script, for example), still possess the meaning of the "thing" or "matter" in question (in the sense of the Latin *causa* or the German *Sache*: the theme or subject matter at issue). But it is particularly instructive, as I see it, to recognize above all that this *sujet*, this *soggetto*, is effectually something that is *proposé*: proposed or nominated—namely something "put forward" or "placed before." We are talking therefore of a proposition, a veritable *pro-posal* for what is properly to be regarded as "being," namely that which enjoys stability, as if we would thereby assert and propose our own permanence—and assert and propose ourselves in terms of this permanence—as if we took time "into our hands" precisely because we would then be laboriously reducing *ta antikeimena* (the circumstances that oppose and resist us) to *hypokeimena*, namely to "things which lie within our power."

This is, of course, a modern reading (where we should point out that we have expressly linked the notions of "hands" and "power," and thus of submitting things to the acting subject). It is a somewhat "violent" reading that accentuates a certain understanding of the *sujet* or *theme* in question here (which is to explore the nature of "the subject" in Hegel), by exploiting those *subjective* hints or traces that are already manifest in the everyday use of certain notable Greek terms and expressions.

Nonetheless, it is worth recognizing that Aristotle, from the beginning, already realized the difficulty of a *substrate* that could propose something for itself, let alone stand as a ground or foundation for mastering whatever opposes it, thus conquering the adversary, so to speak. But in any case it seems that the Stagirite makes this critique of the substrate rather too easy for himself—thus initiating a long philosophical tradition in opposition to materialism—when he identifies *hypokeimenon* and *hylē*, "substrate" and "matter," thereby demoting "that which underlies" to mere *materia bruta* or "material for further development" (and thus, implicitly, fomenting the tendency to convert *ta antikeimena* into *ta hypokeimena*, that is, into things lying at hand or within our reach, things that are *vorhanden* or "present at hand," as Heidegger would say). In this way Aristotle can criticize "the earliest philosophers" who believed that "the principles which underlie all things are only to be found in the realm of matter" (*Metaphysics* I.2, 983b, 6–8), without recognizing something that is indeed obvious to Aristotle (obvious, that is, once the meaning of *hypokeimenon* has been submitted, or "subjected," to that of *hylē*), namely that "is surely not the substrate itself which causes itself to change" (*Metaphysics* 984a, 21–22). Changes transpire in and derive from the substrate, but the latter cannot change in and of itself, for to do so would require the activity of *reflection*—to put this in a specifically modern fashion—or would require us to recognize that the substrate is *destined to be that which it always already was*; would require us to recognize that it *does not go out of itself* in the process of change. On the contrary, it is there where it knows or recognizes itself, where it *uncovers or discloses things in and of itself.*[2]

In step with this transformation of *to hypokeimenon* into something *inert*, something without any life or movement of its own,

Aristotle separates—first in theoretical terms, and then in terms of the "thing itself"—this second principle (the "material cause") from the first and fundamental principle: the ideal agent, the *promoter* of change (the "formal cause" as it was later called). What he goes on to claim is this: "we call one cause the substance [*tēn ousian*] or the 'what it is to be,' or strictly the 'what it was to be' [*to ti ēn einai*], of the thing (since the 'reason why' of a thing is ultimately reducible to its formula [*ton logon*] and the ultimate 'reason why' is a cause and principle)" (*Metaphysics* I.2, 983a, 27–29). We should note the *reflexive* circularity that is expressed here: to say what something *in the last instance* really is, its ultimate *logos*, amounts to affirming all the affections, properties, and determinations of that thing. In other words: everything that constitutes its *being*, what it was in its origin, or what was *inscribed* in it, so to speak, as the "name" that belongs to it in an absolute sense. For what is ultimate, the "ultimate thing" that it is possible to say of something would be its "name": the *name that is proper* to it ("what it was to be," or its *essence*). Thus, in truth, this name would say nothing other, nothing "more," than what *is mentioned or intended by it* (that would be to take it once again as substrate or matter), so that the thing itself would be uttered or expressed, or would utter or express *itself* (in German we could say *Es sagt* rather than *Man sagt*: "It speaks," rather than "one speaks about it"—and this specific qualification is important), would mention or refer to itself, would *itself* name what it was in the beginning and *in principle*, namely *ousia*, or in accordance with the traditional rendering: *substance*. The Greek word *ousia* is a participle of the verb *eimi* and is thus equivalent *to ti ēn einai* ("the what it was to be"). It is by no means unusual therefore for Aristotle to identify *logos* and thing, that which is ultimate and that which is primary *with regard to something*.

And this is certainly not so strange. Yet it remains too easy, for to justify this identification or equivalence we should have to admit, in the first place, the presence of "something" as a *tertium quid*, as a basis common to the name properly speaking and the thing properly speaking, that is, to the *logos* or essence and the *ousia* or substance; namely something *in* which the beginning (the thing) and the end (its name) could recognize one another. And in the second place we should have to demonstrate in this entire *trajectory*—which moves from the beginning to the end: what it will be and what will be said of it, namely its specific determinations—that the thing is thereby effectively realizing its initial *pro-grammē* (in the literal sense of a "prior inscription"), accomplishing that which it already was beforehand. With regard to the first point Aristotle has a response, unsatisfactory though it may be: a response that will sharpen rather than resolve the problem. With regard to the second point, by contrast, "the Philosopher" prefers to dissolve the problem in and at its root rather than attempting to resolve it. Let us start by considering the first point.

How is it possible for word and being, for *logos* and *ousia*, to come together in something, or to be the same thing and be said of the same thing? Aristotle's response to this question, as we have just suggested, sharpens and even *redoubles* the problem rather than resolving it. For he says in effect that *ousia*, or "a substance—that which is called a substance most strictly [*kyriōtata*: 'in the most powerful or pre-eminent degree'—as I would translate it], primarily and most of all—is that which is neither said of a subject [*mete kath'hypokeimenou tinos legetai*] nor exists in a subject [*mete en hypokeimenoi tini estin*]" (*Categories* V, 2a, 11–12). This rather enigmatic and negative definition (in terms of the realm of language and of being alike) is followed by another definition concerning a *secondary* and derived sense of *ousia*: namely the *eidos* (what we see something as and what can therefore be said of it), traditionally rendered as *species* (as well as the *genos* that encompasses a plurality of species). Aristotle says that these species "govern from the beginning," so that we could say that they *underlie (hyparchousin)* the primary substances (cf. *Categories* 2a, 14–16). It is clear therefore that without knowing what these substances are we could not understand them nor could anything even be *said* of them; in other words, it could not be said that there are also secondary substances (i.e., that which is "said" of the primary substances, that which gives them *name and standing* as it were). "The Philosopher" can neither furnish a definition of the *tode ti* (for then he would say something about it) nor demonstrate that it exists (for then they would not be *primary* substances). Thus he must introduce them more obliquely, as examples, employing for this purpose—in somewhat circular fashion—the aforementioned secondary substances or species: "For example, man is said of a subject (*kath'hypokeimenou*), of this individual man (*tinos anthropou*)" (*Categories* 2a, 21–22). Thus *ousia*, in its proper and most authentic sense, is precisely *to hypokeimenon*. In truth, it would not seem necessary to offer an example here (*ontically*, as we might say). It would suffice to resolve (in *logical* terms) the preceding double contradiction into a simple *tautology*: if there is something that is neither said of a subject nor exists in a subject, this is obviously because it is itself the subject, as Aristotle himself concedes (once again obliquely and as something that seems self-evident): "All the other things are either said of the primary substances as subjects or in them as subjects" (2a, 34–35). In short, the real and true *ousia* is this individual concrete thing, and at the same the ultimate subject (*to hypokeimenon eschaton*) of predication in a judgment. Yet we would know nothing about this thing without that "other" *ousia*, the *essence*, or that which is *fully predicated* and *realized*, and which, though it may be separated from the thing in thought, continues to be its *morphē* and *eidos* and governs (*hyparchei*: "falls to" or "belongs to") the *tode tis* in advance.

Here too we can recognize the inseparability of the ontic and the logical dimension. If it is appropriate to deploy the word *ousia*—albeit in a derivative sense—both for the species that expresses "what this individual was from the beginning" and for that which governs it—here too as in the case of the *sub*-stantia which stands *hypo* or "underneath"—this springs from the ambiguity of the Greek word *logos*, which can designate both the enunciation (the judgment in which something is said, *kata tinos*) and the thing that is enunciated. Nonetheless, it is clear that, as the subject of judgment, what is mentioned with this thing (the *tode tis*, "this concrete something") is a mere limit or extreme of the enunciation, a *horismos*, and not the thing in its full range and extent. Regarded from the side of essential predication the subject continues to be submitted or subjected, continues to belong to that determination which "governs it from the beginning." Thus the *hypokeimenon* is contrasted—as if it were the *antikeimenon*—with the *eidos*, which in its predominant action or even assault (*hyparchein*) transforms what is primary or first-born, so to speak, into what is secondary or subordinate, into something or someone that is literally *commanded* (*hyparchos*, according to the French lexicon we have already cited, also signifies: "sujet, soumis à, dependent de"—that which is subject to, submitted to, or dependent on something). In this way, therefore, something that exists *as* the subject *of* an attribute is in turn subject *to* that attribute (that which is primary substance is subject to the *dictio* [enunciation]—and the *ditio* or *dicio* [dominion or authority]—of secondary substance)—if, that is, it would really be something true instead of nothing, or better put, instead of mere *hylē*, instead of that bare *hypokeimenon* of which nothing can be said—precisely because there is nothing to say here.

And this is the source of that double meaning—surviving even today—that attaches to the word "subject": a subject is the one who commands, but also the one who is commanded, a subject of the crown, for example. (In the German of Kant's time the *Untertanen* were still known as *Subjekte*, or subjects of the monarch. The old word *Untertan* expresses the notion of a "subordinate," and, in the most derogatory sense, an "underling.") But to make the problem even more complicated, the agent that "rules" or "commands" cannot be a subject, a *hypokeimenon*, because then this would have to be "matter"—which would be incapable of giving any account of itself or generating its own determinations from out of itself. That which "commands" in the subject—that which tells the subject what it already was—is, as we have seen, the *eidos*, the *species* (or, if we take the word *logos* in its full meaning, the essence: *to ti ēn einai*). Yet secondary substance does not exist of itself, unless it is given with primary substance. We are evidently confronted with a certain inversion here, with an irresolvable chiasmus: that which is first in the order of being is second in the order of logical discourse, and vice versa. As a result, therefore, and strictly speaking, we cannot speak of "ontology" here. It is no accident that one of the first to employ the Latin term *ontologia* (clearly fabricated as a neologism) was a pupil of Descartes, namely Johannes Clauberg.

Until the end of the modern period, "logic" and "metaphysics," technically speaking, will proceed more or less independently. But in truth they are mutually entwined in that uncertain arena or battlefield that the subject has effectively become, as indeed they were in the times of ancient philosophy, when it was already difficult to bring all of these terms and expressions into a fully harmonious or coherent relationship with one another—*hypokeimenon* (substrate or matter in general), *tode ti* (an individual), *protē ousia* (that which in the last instance has to do solely with itself)—in the context of antithetical notions (*to kyriōtaton*, "that which prevails in the greatest degree," on the one hand, and *to hyparchon*, "that which is submitted or subject to its own denominated origin"—its certificate of quality and authenticity, as it were—on the other).

As we can now see, Aristotle does not resolve this problem, but rather accentuates it in the most extreme and desperate manner. We should realize that what is so desperate here is neither logic nor metaphysics as such, but the astonishing circumstance that at one and the same time they are neither separable from one another nor compatible with one another. In effect, Aristotle cannot be satisfied with a *hyparchein* that is merely logical in character to "construct" the world in a rational manner, for it is evident that secondary substance does not exist *in and of itself*: "Man in general would be the principle of man as a universal [*anthropou katholou*], but there is no such man." On the contrary, "the source [*archē*] of individuals is an individual [*to kath'hekaston*]" (*Metaphysics* XII, 1071, a20). In order that the world may exist, therefore, we need an individual source or Principle, and a single one at that, given what Aristotle famously claims by appeal to Homer: "things have no wish to be misgoverned. 'It is not good that many should command: let one alone be the Ruler'" (*Metaphysics* XII, 1076a, 4; cf. Homer, *Iliad*, Bk. II, v. 204). Yet this Monarch for its part cannot be a subject of predication—one can say nothing at all about it—for in that case it would possess features and determinations in common with other subordinate beings (and then it could not itself avoid being "commanded," as we see with the kind of modern Monarch who is therefore regarded—with a greater or lesser degree of cynicism—as "the first servant of the state" in the words ascribed to Frederick the Great). Even less can it be an ultimate subject, for in that case it would be or would involve matter, and would be subject to change. In a word, while it must be an individual, it cannot be a subject. It would therefore have to be *ousia* even though it can never be *ousia*.

Aristotle's name for this contradictory being is "God," which he describes as first or "primary *ousia*," as something that is "simple" in nature, as something that is engaged "in activity" (*kat'energeian*) (*Metaphysics* XII, 1072a, 31–32). But since—let us remember—the *prōte ousia* was defined as *hypokeimenon*, it seems clear that the only way—precarious though it is—of escaping contradiction is to admit another use, an *analogical* one, of the term *prōte*. In his treatise on *The Categories* the word "first" or "primary" signifies that which is "basic," that which "underlies," as in effect befits the ultimate subject of predication (ultimate with respect to discourse, but primary with respect to being: given that there can be nothing below or beneath the *hypokeimenon*—except for the *hypokeimenon* in general: "matter," and not indeed "subject"). In the *Metaphysics* Aristotle's description of divine *ousia* as "primary" possesses a high-ranking axiological status since in effect it governs the series of contraries in the sense that it allows no contradiction within itself (it is absolutely simple). Thus the only conceivable simple principle (although this involves difficulties of its own) would be the individual which is so perfect that it possessed absolutely no need to move or be moved in order to exist, which would then coincide completely and precisely with itself, and only with itself (its definition, its *logos* or essence, would be utterly absorbed in its existing individuality). It would not even be permissible to describe it as a subject or substrate of itself, for that would imply some internal division between its being and its essence). But then what can be said of it at all, even if only by way of analogy? All that can be said is this: *archē gar hē noēsis*—"the principle, in effect, is intellection" (*Metaphysics* XII, 1072a, 30).

For us human beings, *noēsis* (which could also be translated, and with good reason, as "intellectual intuition") is that supreme activity in which the act of thinking and that which is thought instantaneously come together as one. We may speak of "fusion" here, as if we were talking about two separate things that were *then* subsequently united, for as living beings possessed of *logos* (and thus of judgment, of the process that separates subject and predicate, that separates primary and secondary substance) we are thereby *submitted* and *subjected* to time. For all this, it is true—so Aristotle believes—that we too, the philosophers, are capable at least on some occasions of "immortalizing" ourselves in the sense that in an instant "outside of time" *hypokeimenon* and *antikeimenon*, subject and object, can be identified with one another—to return to our earlier terminology—in a simple undivided *actus*. We can thus attribute to God an eternal state of perfection, which, by contrast, "we only rarely enjoy" (*Metaphysics* XII, 1072b, 25). This state of eternal enjoyment, which is at the same time the supreme form of activity (*noēsis noēseōs*), is also described by Aristotle as *zōē* or "life." And indeed, this perfect life, for here the individual coincides absolutely with its species and its genus.

All things considered, the only thing we can definitely say about this supreme life—this Principle, this Individual on which "the sensible universe and the world of nature (*phusis*) depend" (*Metaphysics* XII, 1072b 14), on which the intelligibility and even the existence of the world depend, subject as it is to this single One—is that it negates and destroys, so to speak, in its own excessive character all the forms and schemes of being and of thought that have been so patiently analyzed up until this point.

In effect, for us, God is not intelligible. In and of Himself, or perhaps better: in and of Itself (if we are permitted to intrude on such an intensely focused and concentrated divine existence), the supreme One does not act as an intelligible Individual on anything other than itself (yet what kind of intellection would it have to accomplish if it is indeed already a pure unity of intellection and its intelligible object insofar as the latter is submitted to or is "subject" to the intellect?). Although all things tend toward the supreme One, the latter knows nothing of this, and need know nothing. It is "from without," if we may put it this way, that the supreme One is the ultimate "end" for all things. And yet, in and of itself, the supreme One cannot even be regarded as the end in terms of itself since it has never been separated or divided from itself in the first place. How could that which has always already been the origin or principle possibly be an end? And how can that which never *directly* furnishes the origin or principle for anything turn out to be the ultimate origin and principle, given that other beings move toward it only *hōs erōmenon*, only insofar as it is an object of love? (*Metaphysics* XII, 1072b, 4).

And this is why I claimed earlier that in the last analysis Aristotle dissolved the second problem regarding the relation between the *logos* and the *tode ti* (and *ousia* consisted in just this relation) since the former—we must remember—is an expression of essence if and only if the ultimate definition coincides without remainder with the primary subject, with the *hypokeimenon*. But for that reason, with regard to the whole trajectory, namely the complete path that leads ontically from the origin and principle to the end—the inherence of determinations in the subject—and from which we logically return—with the subsumption of the subject to the predicate—it would be necessary to demonstrate that the journey and the return coincide entirely with one another. It would be necessary to demonstrate, as it were, that the thing in question succeeds in effectively and precisely accomplishing its initial program as we have already described it (in the literal sense of a "prior inscription"), and demonstrate at the same time that the execution of this program succeeds in giving reality, shape, and body to what was previously nothing but substrate, nothing but subject in general: an *x*. Yet, as we have tried to show, Aristotle makes things a little too easy for himself in this regard, for ab initio his supreme principle has no need to go or to return from anywhere. There is no course or trajectory here. Rather, everything that is not God, indeed everything else there is (which is to say: everything that we can think and express and experience) traces its own path inasmuch as it attempts (consciously or not) to conform its life to its definition. And it is precisely because it cannot accomplish this completely that everything here can be called "things" (determinations or properties) that belong to things (qua subjects or individuals). It is precisely for this reason that logical discourse and ontic becoming are given together. Moreover, and also for this very reason, everything—save for God—exists in time, and is thereby destined for death. Only the supreme One lives eternally—as we have had occasion to show—because uniquely God harbors and maintains its essence entire.

Let us briefly recapitulate the argument. We began by showing how the initial problem of metaphysics lay in "counterposing" two modes of "being" or existence: that of the *hypokeimenon* or *subjectum*, and that of the *antikeimenon* or *objectum*. The common use of these ancient terms led us to suspect that the subordination of the second term with regard to the first allowed us to glimpse a primacy, though still latent, of the "subject" here which was sustained and encouraged by this subordinate relation. Our examination of the relevant Aristotelian concepts in this regard, however, yielded a highly ambiguous result, and one that creates more problems than the philosophical tradition has been able to resolve. In the philosophy of the Stagirite the *hypokeimenon* plays, in effect, a double and indeed antithetical role: on the one hand the notion is identified with that of matter or general substrate, while on the other it is identified with individual substance or the subject of attribution. Yet after having laid this basis, the Stagirite sees himself forced to reduce its function and significance to an extreme minimum.

In the first case, matter or the substrate is restricted exclusively to the physical world of becoming (where the notion of the *hypokeimenon* properly served to ensure a certain element of permanence at the heart of change). Above and beyond the realm of matter there lies the purest principle that "erotically" attracts all other beings, without knowing that it does so, and that for its part can somehow, though only obscurely, be conceived as an extremely strange kind of pure and self-activating *morphē*, as something like a secondary substance that would have *subsumed* primary substance entirely without remainder within its own *all-embracing determination*. Yet we would then be talking about an *Eidos* that is alien to the *logos*, one where the *adspectum*—the way in which "it gives itself to be seen"—would be absolutely one with the very act of seeing: the *noēsis*, not of some specific meaning or *noema*, but solely of itself (*noēsis noēseōs*).

In the second case, this same principle sees itself as a perfect inherence of the predicate within the subject: once again we are presented with something that cannot logically be enunciated in terms of any judgment, presented, rather, with what, as something that is simple and true, can only "be apprehended and seen in its (self) manifestation" (*to men higein kai pthanai alēthes*)—as Aristotle says, wrestling with the limits of language—since, as he adds in hermetic parenthesis here, "(for affirmation [*kataphasis*: letting something appear from top to bottom, letting something appear in its place] is not the same as being shown in a flash [*phasis*])" *Metaphysics* IX, 10, 1051b, 24). Moreover, with regard to such a stupendous form of being (though Aristotle still speaks of *ta hapla* in the plural, he soon reveals that there is only one being—God—that is simple and in continual activity (*energeia*), with regard to the supreme One he claims that it is impossible to be deceived. He says that we either "behold and understand" (*noein*) this form of being or we do not (ibid., 1051b, 32), thereby alluding to those rare moments that philosophers are capable of enjoying (the sort of instant in which, as Spinoza would say, *sentimus experimurque nos aeternos esse*).[3] Such is the "immortalization"—rather than immortality—that is available to human beings: an ephemeral *noetic* participation in the divine life, in the *noēsis noēseōs*.

This all rings very well, and sounds indeed "divine" (not unlike the celestial music we have heard for centuries in the course of a less than *holy* union between Scholastic thought and the Christian religion). But it should be clear that rather than resolving the problem of the two senses of *subject* (the subject-thing of *inherence*, and the subject-concept *subsumed* under the predicate), Aristotle has undertaken a flight to the front, as it were, offering as a solution that is nothing more than the forced combination of two approaches in one unique *individual*. And he has done so by suppressing the relation in question. We might therefore be tempted to reject Heidegger's famous judgment on metaphysics as *ontotheology* and argue instead that Aristotle, with his conception of *theos*, actually made it rather difficult to comprehend the connection between the ontical and the logical dimension, or between primary substance as *tode ti*—*hypokeimenon*—and secondary substance as *eidos*—*to ti ēn einai*.

2. Not Substance, But Just as Much Subject

It would of course be extremely misleading to claim that Hegel thinks about the problem of the subject in precisely the same terms that were bequeathed by Aristotle. A long and significant number of famous names, of *intermediary* figures, would clearly document that in this case too we are talking about a certain trajectory in the course of which the problematic we have been discussing is sometimes deepened and enhanced and sometimes obscured. But the very idea of a "closure" with respect to an entire movement of thought—namely "metaphysics"—that has shaped our history (the history of the West), that has thus proved literally epoch-making, would naturally suggest that the thinker who arguably represents the culmination of the metaphysical tradition (and therefore also its decline) must have expended considerable effort on acknowledging and appropriating, in the most thorough and coherent (that is to say: *systematic*) manner, the rich and problematic heritage that began with the thinker who stands at the beginning of that tradition. Nonetheless, going beyond (or rather going back *before*) what he expressly defended as a philosophical *program* with regard to the "demands of the time" and its relationship to the entire earlier development of thought, it is quite clear that Hegel deliberately and repeatedly turns back to ancient philosophy in general, and to Aristotle in particular, precisely to counter the most *recent* aspect of the most *recent* time, namely of Modernity—that is to say: the agnosticism characteristic of the followers of Kant, the egoistic subjectivism of Jacobi, and the unbridled subjectivity of the early romantics, preoccupied as they seemed to be with a hypertrophied and in truth somewhat poignant exhibition of *ego*. And the general significance of what Hegel believed he found in Aristotle, and that he appropriates in his own way, can effectively be described with the single word *relationality*.

For in effect Hegel always thinks in *holistic* terms, in terms of structure, rather than actually attempting to deduce a philosophical system on the basis of a single principle or proposition, as he claimed that Descartes, Reinhold, and Fichte had undertaken to do. Indeed in 1801 Hegel memorably describes the idea that "something merely posited for reflection must necessarily stand at the summit of a system as the highest or absolute or basic proposition" as nothing but a "delusion" (*Wahn*). And shortly after this, in his critical remarks on Spinoza for having begun the presentation of his *Ethics* "with a definition," Hegel claims that the Spinozan philosophy can only properly be reevaluated once "reason has purified itself of the *subjectivity* of reflection." All this clearly reveals his hostility to what he calls the "philosophy of reflection" and the kind of philosophy that typically appeals to "the facts of consciousness," as exemplified by Fichte and his conception of the absolute "ego."[4]

Nevertheless, it is evident that we must recognize a factor that also separates Hegel from Aristotle, and this is the formidable emergence in the Modern Age of a notion of *subject*—one that soon came to dominate the philosophical panorama—which was concerned not only with the human subject qua individual but above all with the "I" conceived as *consciousness*, and, at the same time, as the free subject that is responsible for its own actions. In this regard, it is necessary to mention, at least in passing, the Cartesian "I" that is certain of itself as *fundamentum inconcussum veritatis*, as the unshakeable ground of truth (even if, not altogether coherently, this ground or foundation has to appeal in turn to God). In this respect, we might say, Hegel regards himself as "absolutely modern," so that his criticisms of modern subjectivism should rather be seen as an attack on the uncontrolled desire of the romantics to reduce everything to a fixed point, to a *subject* that is as immovable as it is vain. And for all his reservations in this regard, Hegel will always insist on the importance of the discovery of the infinite value and significance of *interiority* as an essential factor in the experience of freedom.

Thus, if Hegel is prepared to praise Descartes, we must not forget that this is because it was the latter who began to establish "once again" the autonomy of philosophy. For Hegel sees him not so much as an innovator as one who has continued—after the long medieval interruption—what was inaugurated in the great tradition of Greek thought. To take up an image deployed by Hegel himself, it is quite true that the land now glimpsed by the sailor cannot be regarded by him as the same land that he left behind so long before. But what has changed so significantly is not so much the land and the home that it provides (for the fertile soil here is still that of Greece) as the gaze or perspective of the sailor himself, or in other words: the method. Descartes begins in effect by seeking a fixed or stable point, a "concrete this" (*tode ti*) that will serve as a refuge against the mutability of things, and at the same time as a criterion for measuring and comparing the regularity of their changes and movements. And like Aristotle in this, Descartes demands that this point should constitute a *fundamentum*: an ultimate and irreducible subject of predication that cannot be said or predicated of any other *hypokeimenon* and cannot exist in any other *hypokeimenon*, and which in contrast remains and persists within itself. However, we should remember that Aristotle had encountered an obstacle in this regard, that is, the difficulty of having to attribute two antithetical characteristics to the same notion (or at least to the same term, namely the *hypokeimenon*): on the one hand the ground or foundation would have to be regarded as a point (the *prōtē ousia* or individual substance); on the other hand it would have to be regarded as a limitless and amorphous domain (the *hylē* or matter), which would lie at the basis of those same individual substances as *one* of their components (the other being the "form," as we already know).

There is, then, a nest of difficulties and contradictions here that Descartes believed he could resolve by invoking the single word "I." The I, in effect, is a point without extension that moves through time without being modified by any temporal circumstances (and how could it be so modified if it was simple or not made up of parts?). Yet it is certainly *hypokeimenon*, or *fundamentum inconcussum*. But this is not because it could receive determinations within itself (such as secondary substances) that would also belong to other similar individuals, but rather because (and this is the *Cartesian* version of the *transcendental leap*) it constitutes the logical *matter* of all determination (i.e., of the *realitas objectiva* of entities). In this way, the "I" also configures the unlimited *field* of consciousness, something that Aristotle had already suspected when he claimed in *De anima* that "the soul is in some way all things."[5] As far as these "things" are concerned, the "way" this transpires is explained by pointing out that what the soul identifies with is not of course the concrete thing, the *tode ti*, but the *phantasmata* and *noēmata* of things (*De anima*, 431b, 7). And as far as the soul is concerned, what identifies with these "images" and "thoughts" is not the soul as a whole, but rather its active and eternal principle: the *nous* (*De anima*, 431b, 16–17).

In this regard it would not be an exaggeration to say that Hegel does not take a significant step beyond the problems initially addressed by Aristotle and so laboriously pursued and elaborated in the modern age. But what Hegel undertakes to do is nothing less than to gather all these *membra disjecta* of the tradition and transform them into a comprehensive structure, or better, into a "living" organism of thought, converting the ultimate substrate of reality and human life into the purest and complete movement of *self-referentiality*, a movement in which the Subject (if we wish to continue describing it as this) exists for itself and knows itself and nothing but itself—though only to empty or relinquish itself without remainder in and as the Other of itself.[6] For this reason, and in relation those "analytically" minded predecessors incapable of grasping a concrete or organic Whole, Hegel could have adopted as his own the words that Mephistopheles addresses to the student in Goethe's *Faust*:

> Wer will das Lebendige erkennen und beschreiben,
> Sucht erst den Geist herauszutreiben,
> Dann hat er die Teile in seiner Hand,
> Fehlt, leider!, nur das geistige Band.[7]

Hegel will dedicate all his intellectual effort to the task of restoring just this kind of *subjection* between the parts, restoring this kind of *spiritual bond* (rather than restoring the "subject"). And we know of course what he explicitly proposes as his task, according the famous dictum of 1806 from the Preface to the *Phenomenology of Spirit*: "According to my view of things, which can be justified through the exposition of the system itself, everything depends on apprehending and expressing the true not as [*nicht als*] substance, but just as much [*eben so sehr*] as subject."[8]

There is a *vexata quaestio* as to whether something is missing in the first half of the phrase, such as the word *sowohl* (so that it would then read: "not so much as [. . .]"), or a qualifying *nur* (*nicht nur als*: "not only as"). The adverbial *eben so sehr* in the second half of the phrase would seem to demand this latter reading. This would result in a certain leveling of the initial contrast: the true must be apprehended and expressed in the *same* way both as substance *and* subject, and moreover in precisely the same sense. But there are times when philosophy has its reasons of which grammar knows not. And I would therefore argue, however difficult this reading may seem *ad pedem litterae*, that we should accept the phrase just as Hegel framed it. Here there is neither a word too few nor a word too many.

The philosopher begins by assuring us that he has a certain view (*Ansicht*) on things that might initially strike the reader as a particular and *subjective* opinion of his own, for while an individual may honestly be sure and *certain* that the way things are is the way he tells us that *he* sees them, it is always possible to invoke the opinion of some other individual against him. In the end, therefore, it would be necessary to look for some firm and unwavering *fundamentum* or substrate to appeal to. The root of the problem must therefore be sought in the reasons that could be said to arise immanently from *the thing or the matter itself* (*die Sache selbst*), in other words, the reasons to which individual subjects, *velis nolis*, would have to subject themselves and their opinions. But to reach this perspective of a "pure looking on" (*reines Zusehen*), where we only have to "look upon" the thing itself, it is necessary that we relinquish our own particular individuality for the sake of some shared and necessary rule or principle, namely for the sake of a certain *law*.

In this sense, the entire Hegelian philosophy begins with a decidedly *antisubjectivist* gesture. Thus Hegel defines "opinion" as "the way in which an individual thinks and represents things to himself in a merely subjective and arbitrary [*subjektive, beliebige*] manner."[9] And in effect, even if this is far from certain etymologically speaking, it looks as if the word for "opinion" itself—as expressed in German of course: *die Meinung*—would seem to emphasize the purely individual "I" (*eine Meinung ist mein*—an opinion is mine after all or what I "mean" is "mine"—as they say), and in this sense cannot therefore aspire to any general or universal validity. And that is why Hegel demands that the individual be prepared to *sacrifice* his own particularities in order to allow the Thing itself, or the Matter which is in question here (i.e., *le sujet*), to reveal or manifest itself: to unfold *in and of itself* without any external interference whatsoever. But the Thing or Matter is not in turn something that is merely *objective*, if by "objective" we understand something that is alien or external to the human subject—for then, on the contrary, all of our attempts to know or act with regard to it would prove vain and fruitless (as in effect is the case with the Kantian *thing in itself* according to Hegel). Rather, it necessary for us to recognize and include in some way the capacities (practical and cognitive) of these very subjects which are also specifically required to abstain from intervening externally. Hegel's name for that which integrates "reflection" and "unfolding" (or immanent development) is "concept" (*Begriff*)—a word that in this case is perhaps actually more appropriate in Spanish (*concepto*) than it seems in German, given that it refers essentially to an all-encompassing *conception* or *comprehension* of something.[10] Hegel tells us that "philosophical thinking reveals itself as the activity of the concept itself." And he continues, emphasizing the abnegation of the individual subject that specifically interests him in this connection, as follows: "For this expressly demands the effort to free ourselves of our own whims and particular opinions which constantly threaten to reappear."[11]

For the sake of argument, let us provisionally accept that Hegel really does wish to say what he seems to be telling us here: that we must regard our single and particular "I" as a *quantité négligeable*, as something entirely evanescent, and thus allow consciousness (something that we all possess, although it would not in any way be peculiarly "our own," as also seems the case with Kant's "transcendental subject") to establish solely through itself the agreement or "adequation" of reality (the represented object) with the concept (the power of representation itself, as we might say).

We ourselves—as mere cognitive points of reference—would have to look on or contemplate (to apprehend) the whole process "from without," and in the best case would thereby be allowed to express the latter in its own terms. In short, it is necessary to be objective and to say things as they are. Is this not just what Hegel wants to tell us with all of these admonitions to *mortify* the individual? But if it were so, how are we to capture and express the truth, if for Hegel "the true is the whole"? Would there not then be *two things* in play?—on the one hand we ourselves, those who merely "look on" or contemplate (who, even reduced to points of view— surely the perfect phrase here—would have to enjoy an existence of some kind) and that which is contemplated "in truth" (namely that *reflection* on itself that consciousness undertakes to identify itself with the object in its role as the criterion of truth: as concept?)

Following Fichte, and internally assuming what for Fichte constituted the starting point of all activity (the *I* or *absolute subject*),

Hegel concedes of course that the beginning of philosophy has to be found in a negative activity, one that is *purified* of everything merely finite, but one that as such must be absolutely *abstract* and *empty* since it negates all that it itself is not—and that means Everything, starting with one's own individual "subjective I" and everything that transpires within it. In this way this *abnegation*, this self-negation of the individual finite subject, is already the *self-positing* of the universally concrete infinite subject. Let us remember that in the famous formulation in the Preface to the *Phenomenology*, Hegel specifically demands that we *express* the true as Subject. But not indeed because there are somehow three "things" here: the finite subjects, the Subject, and the expression of the latter by the former. The finite subjects *already are themselves* that expression. And the infinite Subject (if we still wish to describe it in these terms, in accordance with the terminology deployed in the Preface to the *Phenomenology*) exists and recognizes itself precisely in and through that expression, and not outside of it.

Thus, the truly significant thing here, Hegel's decisive contribution to the problem of the subject, lies in the way he does not propose a new solution in this regard, as if the two extremes of the Aristotelian alternative (the *eidos* and the *hypokeimenon*) needed to be replaced. To put this succinctly in traditional terminology: on the one hand we have *form*, that which is determining and bestows determinacy, and on the other we have *matter*, that which can be determined and rendered determinate). If this is how things stand it is easy to recognize that the mistake would lie in exclusively emphasizing one of these sides, in reducing the other one to itself, either to declare that it is unknowable, something that exists solely *in itself*, or to regard matter as being *ultimately identical with form* (logically speaking all judgments would then be reduced—at least for the Divine Mind—to a single *identical judgment: Noēsis noēseōs*, "A = A," "I think therefore I am," "I = I"—so many empty formulas for the same thing.).

To escape this sterile alternative Hegel simply notes that the "relation to objects," this activity without which the subject could never have come to recognize itself as pure *relation-to-self* (there can be no *self-consciousness* without consciousness of something, without intentionality) alters both the subjective activity of thinking and the status of the object envisaged. The thinking of truth, the thinking that brings truth, is always a *rethinking, a thinking over* something (*ein Nachdenken*), a reflection "*upon* something." But that which is "reflected" here is neither of the two extremes but rather the *very relation* between both! But the *simple relation-to-self* is thereby transformed into a double movement: that which appears, namely *form*, is obviously the *appearing* (*Erscheinung*) of the substrate. This latter does not lie sequestered somewhere else or hidden somewhere underneath, untouched and unknowable, but rather "gives itself to be seen"—in a very Greek sense—*in* its own *phenomenon* (a word that signifies nothing but "that which gives itself to be seen").

3. The Reflexive Movement of Thinking

What this movement of reflection furnishes are thus the "thoughts" *of* things and not merely *my* thoughts. It is not that thoughts "belong" to two regions: that of the external world and that of my mind. On the contrary, it is the world and the mind that acquire *meaning* in the reflexive movement of thinking. In this regard Hegel offers a very simple example: "Nature shows us an infinite amount of individual shapes and phenomena. We have a need to introduce unity into this manifoldness. Hence we compare and seek to recognize the universal in each case."[12] Thus what is *essential* here (again the perfect expression) is to recognize that this "unity," which does not thereby cease to be a product of our spirit, is in precisely the same sense (*eben so sehr*, we might say) universality, or the authentic significance and "value of the *basic matter* [*Sache*], the *essential*, the *inner*, the *true*."[13] The thoughts, therefore, without ceasing to be "the *product of my spirit* insofar as the latter is a thinking subject,"[14] and indeed precisely *because* it is such a product, are also "*objective* thoughts"[15] that furnish "consciousness with the *true* nature of the *object*."[16]

If this is indeed so, then the age-old distinction between logic and metaphysics now loses its meaning: "*Logic* thus coincides with *metaphysics*, i.e. the science of *things* captured in *thoughts* that have counted as expressing the *essentialities of things*."[17] The task of the *Science of Logic* will thus consist in *sublating* or transcending this age-old opposition between the subjective and the objective, but without thereby collapsing into some "point of indifference," without seeing this very movement of conciliation as the only thing that can properly be described as the "the Self-Same": not in order to exclude its "Other" but rather to be and exist freely in this Other, in its own alterity as *Nature*. Hence the *ternary* rhythm of what Hegel calls the "logical element" (*das Logische*). And this explains why the *Science of Logic*—in accordance with the opposition we have mentioned—is divided into two parts: the *objective* logic and the *subjective* logic, although it consists of three books. Or to put this in the Aristotelian terms that we have been taking as our guiding thread here: the Hegelian Whole, the fully true and the only truth (everything else is at best merely probable or "correct" by comparison) is the completely exhaustive display or unfolding of "primary substance" (at once subject and substrate: namely *being*) up to the point where it can be identified, without remainder, with "secondary substance" (namely *essence*, for which being is *its very appearance*), to the point where we also recognize that the absolute inhesion of the latter in the former just is, without remainder, the full expression of the subject in *its* object (the *concept* that can only conceive itself in conceiving its Other). To put this more precisely: (1) the unfolding of being, the movement out of itself through which it determines itself as "*what* it already was" (namely essence, emphasizing the *quod*, the *substrate*), constitutes the *logic of being*: the passage or transition from being—and from the determinations *kath'auto* which distinctively belong to being—into essence; (2) the inhesion, the unfolding of essence within itself through which it finds itself reflected as "what it already *was*" (this time, by contrast, emphasizing *existence*), is nothing but the enfolding of essence into *itself*, into its single character as substrate-in-movement; and that *double reflection* (a self-relationship indeed, not merely a unilateral relation of one thing to another) is what constitutes the *logic of essence*; (3) the *development* of the "self-same" here involves and implies: (a) its immediate appearing as such, that is to say, as a subject for which objects would exist (the Doctrine of *Subjectivity*), (b) the *externalization of itself* as object (the Doctrine of *Objectivity*); and (c) the perfect interpenetration of Subject and Object, or as we might say, of being and essence, once each has externalized and interiorized itself in its Other (the *Idea*).

I think that now, finally, we should be in a position to understand the meaning of the famous "program" that Hegel presents in the Preface to the *Phenomenology of Spirit*. We have already emphasized the necessity of providing a *literal* reading of the passage in question, in spite of the awkward (not to say, grammatically incorrect) character of Hegel's actual form of linguistic expression here. With Hegel himself, therefore, we should remember that with the full development of the system (a *self-moving* development in which *we* are able to recognize ourselves rather than simply being eliminated through the evolution of the Concept), it is necessary for us to *apprehend* and *express* the True (the Whole) *not* as substance, but *eben so sehr* as subject.

4. The Unveiling of Substance as the Genesis of the Concept

In the first place Hegel clearly presents us with an emphatic negation: substance *is not* (yet) the True. Regarded as *substrate*, both in the Aristotelian sense and in the much more complex sense of Spinoza (for in the latter case substance is conceived not only *in se*, in itself, but also conceived *per se*, through itself), it is true that substance *sensu lato* naturally constitutes the properly *philosophical*—namely *reflexive*—*beginning of philosophy*.

Indeed, from the beginning, and as such, being is considered *essentially* as *simple relation to itself* (*einfache Beziehung auf sich*). But now, as we have indicated, that *relation determinately negates* its own determinations (namely the thoughts insofar as they presented themselves as *merely subjective forms*—logical principles and categories—that are to be applied to a reality that is alien and external to them). Essence *negates itself* as something merely "inner" over against the *appearances of the world*, and is thus—without recognizing this for its part—the entirety of those appearances that, through being appearances of essence itself (rather than of a world "elsewhere," of a world that would then be inessential), thereby cease to be mere "appearances" and become its own *proper* appearing.[18] *Das Wesen muss erscheinen*: "*Essence cannot but appear*" (*WdL. GW* 11, 323). And this, of course, is just how the second section of the *Logic of Essence* begins.

However, the subject is not something that is somehow added to substance: it is the relation of substantiality itself that, considered completely *solely in and for itself*, leads *of necessity* to its contrary: namely the *free* concept (see *WdL. GW* 12, 15), which is liberated from any bond or fetter (for it *is* that which binds: the spiritual bond, though still considered here in an abstract way). Hence the *unveiling* of substance *is already* the *genesis* of the concept (ibid.). And since the "I" is nothing but the actual existence (*Dasein*) of the concept, it follows that *substance is the nature of the I*, that the latter issues from the former and expresses—as a result of its unfolding and unwinding—the truth of substance. A truth that exhibits, however, a double character: as *self-referential unity* the concept now returns *freely* to the *self-sameness* of being as *substrate*. Now, finally, "primary substance" is entirely subsumed in "secondary substance," or in universality. But this universality is indeed *concrete* since it bears and holds all particularity and all individuality within itself. It is concrete, but it does not yet know that it is. And for that reason, the concept, inasmuch as it is the immediate result of substance, does not yet know itself as being the Self-same, know itself as the True, that is say, as the Whole. Of course, it does know itself in a sense, but only as something *different* from external things (from what Fichte would call "being"). But such thinking still only expresses "subjectivity or the formal (*formellen*) concept" (see *WdL. GW* 12, 30). In other words: at this level the subject still thinks of itself as *substance*, namely as something *inner*, as "thing in general," for which or in relation to which everything else—that is, the non-I—exists.

That is why we are told, in the Preface to the *Phenomenology*, that the True is *not* to be expressed as Substance, while we are nonetheless also specifically told that since the subject, and only the subject, is the True it is so *exactly in the same sense* as we have seen that substance is in its *absolute reflection*, that is to say, precisely as Subject. For the *nature of the subject is substance*. Thus, the subject, as that which has issued or resulted from substance, is indeed "being in and for itself, but is so, at first, for us or *in itself* [. . .] and it must also be so *for itself*" (cf. *WdL. GW* 12, 30).

> [. . .] facilis descensus Averno;
> noctes atque dies patet atri ianua Ditis;
> sed revocare gradum superasque evadere ad auras,
> hoc opus, hic labor est.[19]

This is the challenge, and this the difficulty. The subject has to be for itself "what it already was," that is to say, essence or substance. But without having to forfeit all determinate character, or in other words: without ceasing to be *relationality*, to be pure movement, or a paradoxical sort of *self-moving substance*. In this form of knowing, in this *self-knowing*, the opposition or duality between essence and existence, between the past and *its* future, between the possible and the contingent, also falls away. All that remains is the *necessity* itself of this entire conception, that is to say, the *concept* of such *self*-recognition in a double alterity. Such is the *intrinsic* development (neither simply exterior nor merely interior) of the *subjective logic*. What was once said of the restless *phusis* of Heraclitus may thus also be said of the Concept: that in changing—in changing *its* Other and thus changing *itself* in this change—it rests. Or rather, that here change is rest, the conclusive identification of thought as being and being as thought. This is, at first and immediately, "that which is free and autonomous, the subjective which determines itself in terms of itself, or rather the *subject* itself." Pure negativity that is at the same time *self-affirmation*, then? Indeed, but only if this self-affirmation transpires in the Other of itself will the subject also be the *living substance* of all reality, namely the Idea as a "return to life"; and yet, in assuming or sublating this "objective" dimension in and for itself, the subject will also, and above all, remain "impenetrable atomic subjectivity."[20]

5. Begging the Question of Beginning

Is this, then, the last word of the *Science of Logic*, namely that the Absolute is Subject? Absolutely not. The very *thematic* position of the subject reveals its *relational* character (between "actuality" or *Wirklichkeit*, the examination of which forms the culmination of the "Logic of Essence," and the "Doctrine of Objectivity": the truth of the subject merely as formal concept). For we should remember that the Subject is to be apprehended *in the same sense* as substance, yet not as substance. And the "Subjective Logic" itself? Does it not sum up and bring the whole course and development of the "*logical element*" to a close? Indeed, it does. But only for the Idea to give itself or release itself (*sich entlassen*) freely in and as Nature.[21] But we are suddenly confronted with a rather disturbing suspicion here: would the whole *Logic* itself not then involve a kind of *mediation*, a regression to nature, a highly articulated and deliberate one, just as at the beginning the beginning had to begin with completely *unconscious nature*? From the perspective of finite spirit, from the perspective of each one of us, the unconscious activity of the subject can be understood as "the night of the I." This is the absolute and universal void "which harbours everything within itself," yet inters "a whole world of representations" within this *bottomless pit*.[22] The "I" emerges from its "night"[23] in *thinking over and thinking back upon* (*nachdenken*) those representations, allowing the truth of things to shine forth in them—once they have been transformed into thoughts—and the truth of itself as well. Does not Hegel himself recognize that there is a kind of *unconscious logic* at work here? For he explicitly tells us that "the thought determinations which pervade our spirit in an unconscious and instinctive way, and which even as they emerge in language are not considered or taken as objects of thought,"[24] so that the *Science of Logic* could not even exist without the *reconstruction* (ibid.) of those same determinations. But if that is so, whence do they arise in the first place, what is their origin and *nature*, a nature which of course precedes the "I" in every one of us?

Is there not perhaps a Night that is deeper and more ancient than the night of the "I" itself, a thick and murky night that resists or evades the all-inclusive demands of the system?[25] If it is indeed true, in the "quantum leap" of the Idea toward Nature or as Nature, that this latter is nothing but a kind of "deject" or "falling away," an *Abfall*, of the Idea itself, a paradoxically *total* residuum, relic, or remainder of the Whole, of the Subject,[26] will the Idea be capable of recuperating itself from this dejection or falling away, even if at the end of the day it has proved capable of *recognizing itself* and unfolding its own riches *concretely* as spirit?

For if Nature is the *total remainder*, the absolute remains, of the Idea, what exactly is the source of "the impotence [*Ohnmacht*] of nature to *hold fast* [we could say: *submit*) to the concept [*festzuhalten*] in the unfolding of this latter."[27] Why is it that nature can only "maintain the determinations of the concept in an abstract manner"?[28] How can the ultimate Subject, namely Spirit, know its own self as the *Absolute* in and for itself if it cannot fully exercise dominion over its own Nature (in all senses of this word), and this not because the latter is somehow opposed to it, but rather because the Subject *sinks and founders* in the bottomless depths of a Night which is prior the "I," which indeed is prior to God Himself: that Life which lives solely in its own right, that Knowing which knows itself, and knows itself only in its own Other, but which does not know *whence it itself arises*, steeped as it is in its own nocturnal darkness? And is that pure and perfect movement capable, in truth, of returning entirely into its Self? What is that "Self-Same" that can also exemplify its creeping and elusive remainder, or somehow constitute its own remains?

Here, at the end of the road, I am unable to say anything further, and can only summon the strength to finish—endowing them with another and literally *mortal* sense—with the words which were placed at the end of Spinoza's unfinished *Tractatus de intellectus emendatione*:

RELIQUA DESIDERANTUR.

Here I would like to translate this, in my own way, as "the remainder remains unsaid."

Chapter II

Hegel on the Death of Christ
(Ich bin der Kampf selbst)

1. The Infinite Value of Subjectivity

The thought of Hegel turns obsessively on a certain impossible conjunction, a contradiction that we cannot fully absorb or take upon ourselves, the irreconcilable character of which may nonetheless be said to constitute our "Occidental" identity. This is the contradiction between the need for spiritual signs that would allow us to believe that we are "chosen" and "cherished," that we are embraced and protected by a Heavenly Power that was unknown to us until now, and the demand for a form of "wisdom" that would allow us to know ourselves, to comprehend the earth and the human beings who inhabit it, in order to turn the driving whirlwind of the abyss toward the heights of the "I" that orders or dis-poses all things, that surpasses or transcends all things, this center of attraction that at once reunites all things and defines them in their very singularity.

Hegel's thought stands at the crossroads, at the point of intersection between the abstractly universal law of Judaic rootlessness (*Bodenlosigkeit*) and the concrete rootedness (*Bodenständigkeit*) of Greek *Póleis*. And it is clear—from his own earliest stubborn attempts to reconcile the demands of a mythology of reason and a sensual religion (*Volksreligion*), up until the final Berlin lectures of 1831, which are torn between the need to expound religion as the ethical foundation of the State in the world and the rival contemporary temptation to seek refuge in an otherworldly supernaturalism—just how intensely Hegel struggles to find the most appropriate means of properly understanding the significance of Christianity. And this whole undertaking, in all rigor, is preeminently concerned with unraveling the meaning of those strange and difficult words that speak of something hybrid, uncanny, and monstrous: "For the Jews require a sign, and the Greeks seek after wisdom: but we preach Christ crucified, unto the Jews a stumbling block, and unto the Greeks foolishness; but unto them which are called, both Jews and Greeks, Christ the power of God, and the wisdom of God. Because the foolishness of God is wiser than men; and the weakness of God is stronger than men."[1]

Nothing would be easier, nothing would be more "Greek" in the Pauline sense, than to try to shirk this manifest contradiction by appealing to the need for any number of careful distinctions and qualifications here. Thus, the believers, those "which are called," would know that what must appear as "foolishness," as a "scandal," to the "Others" is itself, in truth, power and wisdom. However, in the first place, the Call here is truly catholic or universal in character. For with regard to the Divine Voice, to the Verbum, there no longer are any "Others." Nevertheless, if there are still some people who refrain from hearing the Word, it is because they really refuse to understand. There is no blindness here, but only a willful averting of the gaze; there is no "hardening of the heart" through the deed of Jahweh, but only a stubborn and unyielding refusal to accept the Word. And, in the second place, we are forced to think that the power of God is his weakness, that the wisdom of God is his foolishness. And this is what they intrinsically are "in themselves" or, which is the same thing, what they are "for us." It is the lack of resistance to all worldly power that makes this weakness something that is all-powerful. Against this weakness it is quite impossible to struggle, not, however, because it somehow withdraws into the security of a "world beyond," but because its emptiness reveals that the gesture of the Adversary was only the result of an earlier emptiness. And it is the foolishness of Christ crucified that already consigns to failure any attempt to provide an intelligible response (i.e., a universal and necessary response) to the question framed by the demands of wisdom, namely: what is truth?

The only possible response to this question arises from an insoluble contradiction, the contradiction that is the "I": "I am the Way, the Truth, and the Life." But how can the cross planted on Golgotha be itself a way or path? And how could the Truth (i.e., that which is universal and necessary) be a single witness to utter desertion and abandonment by the universal Father?

How can Death itself be Life? And yet, would it even be possible to think of something like a Way without the Cross that centers and localizes every horizon? Would we be able to articulate any truthful propositions without the confidence to presuppose the "I" that, without being itself true, "must be able to accompany all of my representations"?[2] Is death the "contrary" of life, as a prudent and reverent Socrates imagined in the *Phaedo*? Or is it not, rather, for the living being—and preeminently for the human being who, being mortal, possesses some knowledge of this—that death and life are the two directions that belong to the one self-same path? Thus, Novalis came very close, in his poetic way, to something that would bring our human understanding to its own destruction. Appealing to Christ, and calling him by the name that he truly is, the "Singer" who has traveled to Palestine does not recount that the Child, this Child, will come to die in the future (although, for the time being, he lives still). He tells us, rather: *Du bist der Tod, und machst uns erst gesund* ("Thou art Death, who alone dost make us Sound").[3]

In this connection it is important to bear in mind that it is not the death of Christ that saves us, but the death that *is* Christ. But what does it save us from? "It saves us precisely from the desire for salvation, from that desperate and imperious desire for salvation which identifies itself with the desire for life, with the thirst for existence. Salvation lies in the renunciation of salvation," according to the rather Schopenhauerian-sounding observations of Andrea Emo.[4] Nonetheless, in spite of the extreme proximity of the fundamental questions that all these writers raise in this regard, I believe that Hegel's position here is actually more disturbing, more tragic, than either Novalis or Emo. More disturbing and tragic than the former, for the poet here projects a conception of Christianity as a kind of serene and untroubled ocean into which all of the aspirations, presentiments, and yearnings of the other religions ultimately feed and where they finally come to rest. Thus we sense here that a certain paradoxical belief in "progress" on the part of the romantic poet ends up with a "Platonizing" reading of Christianity that turns it into a *praeparatio mortis*, into a *Sehnsucht nach dem Tode*, a yearning for death, and beholds in death itself the promise of everlasting rest and tranquility. And again, more disturbing and tragic than Emo because—with a violently "Orientalizing" twist—he proclaims the self-dissolution or self-annihilation of the individual as such, whereas Hegel argues that "I, as this individual, do not wish, nor ought I, to perish or go under [*zugrundegehen*] in the pursuit of my ends. This is my *interest*."[5]

In his final Berlin period Hegel patiently delivered a series of lectures on the philosophy of religion once every two or three years (in 1821, 1824, 1827, 1829, and 1831), all conceived and executed in very close connection with his other lectures on logic and metaphysics. And these lectures on the philosophy of religion all stand under a common denominator: it is thought alone that distinguishes the human being from other beings. It is above all in the medium of thought, then, that we must give honor to and find the appropriate dwelling for the Supreme One: the task is to raise the images and representations of God to the level of thought, and thereby to raise ourselves as well to the activity of genuine thinking itself. The ultimate end and purpose, and—strictly speaking—the only end and purpose of philosophy is "to know and comprehend the religion that *exists*" (*die Religion, die IST, zu erkennen und zu begreifen*).[6] To think existence, to think that which is—this is the general program Hegel undertakes to fulfill. Not to seek refuge in the interiority of the soul while declaring that everything exterior is unknowable or undesirable, or something that might be exchanged for some dreamed-of future. Rather, the task is to *do what has to be* (and can be) *done*, and also (which is the same thing) to *know what is said*.

For this reason, in the various lecture courses on the philosophy of religion that he delivered in Berlin, Hegel invariably begins with what he calls the *concept* of religion. In this context the relevant "concept" is to be understood as an intermediate stage between what he somewhat figuratively describes in the *Phenomenology of Spirit* as the "mere concept" and the emphatically concrete and one and only *Begriff* of the *Science of Logic*, the Concept that does not permit any further qualifications precisely because they have all already been "sublated" (*aufgehoben*) or absorbed within itself. In the context of the lectures "concept" must be understood in the sense of a precise kind of "thought" (*Gedanke*): a conceptual determination that is infinite with regard to its form (as a pure result of thinking) but is still limited with regard to its content. Nonetheless, it is perhaps conceivable that one might reproach Hegel here precisely because the initial concept that he seeks appears so reminiscent of specific themes and attitudes that are already characteristic of the Christian faith itself that we cannot help suspecting that they are derived from it in the first place, rather than arising from the supposed concept of "religion in general." And this suspicion is well founded. Yet this should be regarded less as a reproach than as a sign of Hegel's specific methodical procedure. It is only natural that the initial concept results from the abstraction and generalization of characteristic features of the Christian religion. For how could he proceed otherwise? Perhaps from a dispassionate or "scientific" observation of all the religions there have ever been?—in the style of a watered-down ecumenism where all religions are "equal in the eyes of God," to paraphrase Ranke's famous saying that all historical epochs are equally close to God. And how could we know that these doctrines are justified in claiming genuine religious content for themselves if we did not possess some measure or yardstick beforehand that would allow us to make the relevant comparisons? How could we escape from the circle involved here—or rather, how could we enter the circle properly in the first place—without accepting something in advance, without the prejudice in favor of the religion of the people to which we ourselves belong, of the tradition in which we already find ourselves situated, which furnishes the standard from which to judge the religious value or significance of other faiths or confessions? It is just that this prejudice must come in turn to justify itself genetically, that is, by showing how this religion, the Christian religion, emerges from the progressive dialectical negation and development of a *determinate* series of religious outlooks and confessions (or better: of religious visions of the world as such). Or, and this amounts to the same thing, considered from the inverse perspective of the lectures, we have to show how the abstract concept of the lectures splits or comes asunder, how it passes out of itself and displays itself in and through time (even as it also "scans" the movement of different times, given that all religion, in its beginnings, is regarded *a tergo* as the supranatural foundation of time). In a genuinely hermeneutical circle (or better: a spiral) of retroduction, the basic features of Christian doctrine are read, or better: are "translated" into the abstract language of logico-ontological conceptuality. From the existing religion of Christianity we extract the concept (initially only the subjective concept) of religion; in tracing how this concept is externalized and "dirempted" in specific temporal forms—forms that are preserved dialectically as necessary "moments" of the truth—we find we have returned concretely to the Christian religion: the result of this self-determination is *eo ipso* the foundation of the initial concept. At no point or moment of this process have we abandoned the rational structure of the Christian religion. However, the reverse is also true: if that structure was regarded as rational, this itself was justified through (was deduced from) a threefold process: (1) in an external and empirical sense through the completion of the entire series of religious configurations; (2) in an internal sense through the development of the religious consciousness up to the point where it knows and recognizes itself as self-consciousness or spirit, that is to say, where it sees itself as free subjectivity; (3) in a speculative sense through the systematic development or unfolding of realized knowing, a development in which, as we shall see, the logical path (that of the Idea) and the phenomenological path (that of self-consciousness) come harmoniously together.

2. The Death of Christ and the Commencement of History

"'When the time has come, God sent forth his Son'; and *that* the time had come can only be discerned from history" (*V-Rel.* 5, 147; Hodgson 3, 215). What this interpretation of *Galatians* (ch. 4, v. 4) directly confronts us with is not a justification of the advent of Christ through history but the reverse: the justification of history through the Advent of Christ. It is the latter that grounds the notion of "fulfilled time," the time in which spirit, through its immanent and necessary development, knows and recognizes its own manifestation and externalization, and knows and recognizes itself as such. The self-emptying (*kenosis*) of the Incarnation is precisely a "Being-at-Home-with Oneself-in-the-Other": the Annunciation of Freedom. Time is founded, and offers a foundation, only when it begins to turn toward Spirit: only there where the fellowship and intercommunication of spirits institutes community, sets limits to nature, and defines its role and significance.

In effect, the role—the logically necessary function—of Christianity lies in the mutual unification and transformation of the vanished beauty of the Greek world, at once sullied and universalized by Rome, and the awesome but empty sublimity that is revered by Jerusalem: *Allheit* or Totality (the Greco-Roman Pantheon) versus *Allgemeinheit* or Universality (the formless sublimity of the Hebrew God). And the center of this double movement of mediation (the descent of God to man/the ascent of man to God) lies in a Nature that is blemished, in a particularity that is subsumed by *universality* (the obedience of the Son toward the Father as a determining judgment, following the Kantian example of *casus datae legis*[7]), and in which *singularity* now inheres (Christ—and with him every human being—as the vessel of Spirit, in the relevant sense that singularity can only present itself in a *particular* subject: Jesus of Nazareth, for example, who spoke the Aramaic language, who lived in the time of Herod and Pontius Pilate, etc.). This chiasmus, this union of the logic of subsumption and the logic of inhesion in the middle term that is Christ (which acknowledges and localizes of everything that was natural in other previous religions) implies in a concrete and determinate fashion that it is only the death of Christ (the death of Nature in Christ) that allows the Father to pass, without remainder, over into Spirit, or—to put the same thing in the language of the *Encyclopaedia*—allows the passage from the element of the Logical (*das Logische*) to the Spirit of the community. It is this death and transfiguration that is celebrated in the sacrifice, in the *cultus*, with the ingestion and consumption (the physical destruction) of the bread and wine (of the flesh and blood of the Redeemer) through the Word of the Rite (the incarnation of the logical moment: the realization of the concept) that is accepted and acknowledged by the Community of the Faithful, by the *Gemeinde*.

This is the syllogism of the "consummate religion": the universal (thought) imbues the singular (the moment of the cultus: the truth of ethical life) by the mediation of the particular (the moment of representation: the figure of Christ who has passed away and is in each case brought back to life).[8] The death of the Redeemer is at the same time the liberation of human beings, in the higher society of the *Gemeinde*, from their subjection to nature. This is the profound significance of Christianity according to Hegel's interpretation: the absolute desacralization and profanation of the earth in the name of and by virtue of the God-Man. *The sacred dies at the hands of the sanctified one*: cultivation, culture, cult: three moments of the progressive taming or domestication of all that is alien and hostile—at the cost of transforming the everlasting and firm-set seat of Gaea, the earth, into a wasteland. Christianity turns the earth into something inhospitable, for its "Kingdom is not of this world," although it certainly manifests or presents itself—and this is the characteristic Hegelian twist or torsion—only in (the idealization of) this world.

Of course, a whole series of disturbing and disconcerting questions well up at this point, questions that can only be discussed in a rather summary form here. If the Father is the representational expression of abstract thought, of the metaphysical concept, where, we must ask, has this concept been abstracted from? What precisely is its place of origin, if it ends up standing "beyond the physical," beyond *phusis* or nature? What is it, in short, that bestows blood and strength on this syllogistic and religious movement of thought/representation/and *cultus* of the community? At what cost—at the cost of what—is this reconciliation between the Father and the Spirit produced and celebrated? What is it that dies with Jesus, and proves incapable of resurrection? It would be too easy to respond to all this with the word "Nature." For, within the economy of the encyclopedic system, nature is the *Abfall*, the castoff, as it were, of the Idea[9] and the result of the *logos*, and at the same time the presupposition, the ground that has emerged as the field or arena for the activity of spirit.[10]

If such a nature is by definition susceptible to domestication (given its logical origin in the Idea), there must also be a ground that has not emerged into the light, some obscure and hidden ground or source. Something that admits no such domestication or discipline (*Zucht*): a death that does not die, that is to say, a death that admits no such transfiguration, a kind of opaque sound without reverberation.

Friedrich Hölderlin, more tragic and audacious than his one-time friend (and whom Hegel would soon abandon to his fate), describes this strange power that always prevails, this powerful source of supply, specifically as *Natur*[11]; yet also, in a deeper and more appropriate way, as *Nacht*[12] (Night), precisely to avoid any conflation with that "nature" that has been entirely subdued and made disposable for our purposes, that is simply "present at hand," and again as *heiliges Chaos* ("sacred chaos")[13] and *uralte Verwirrung* ("primeval confusion").[14] But above all, its authentic name is *heiliges Wildnis* ("sacred wilderness").[15] The word *Wildnis* (the etymological source of *Wald*: "wold" and "wood" in English, *hyle* or timber in Greek, *silva* in Latin—related to *salvaje, selvaggio, sauvage, savage*) names that which precedes all culture and cultivation, all *cultus*, and resists them all. The "uncultivated," then, but not the desert, the wasteland (the place of the devil, the ape of God, and thus the inversion of religion, but still ultimately a form of religion), but rather what is teeming, verdant, and luxuriant: that inexhaustible *chora*, always lurking beneath the *urbs*, indeed within the City itself, hidden in the opacity of stone and the smooth mobility of skin, in the moist gaze of the eye and the dark recesses of sexuality. It is something that does not allow of further clarification or elaboration, the contrary of the Eucharistic bread and wine, so susceptible to symbolism, and so conceptually transparent. It is the savage and the unconscious, that which remains refractory to *Logos*, Nature, and Spirit.

It is this ominous latency or potency that renders the fulfillment of the Hegelian program so difficult: the task of somehow overcoming time (*das Tilgen der Zeit* of which Hegel speaks in the *Phenomenology of Spirit*), or what comes to the same thing: of reaching the point where *der Geist in allem, was im Himmel und auf Erden ist, sich selbst erkenne* (where "spirit shall recognize itself in everything in heaven and on earth"). Nonetheless, in a certain respect Hegel is quite right when he immediately goes on to emphasize that *Ein durchaus Anderes ist für den Geist gar nicht vorhanden* (in a literal translation: "There is nothing at hand that is wholly alien to spirit").[16] That which is absolutely Other eludes all presence by definition. But that does not mean that its secret power is any less turbulent, given that this "blind multiplicity which is bereft of the concept"[17] threatens to frustrate the programmatic intentions of the Preface to the *Phenomenology of Spirit*, namely that of apprehending and expressing substance precisely as subject.[18] The disturbing flaw or fleck here is, of course, branded by Hegel as the *Ohnmacht der Natur* ("the impotence of nature").[19]

Yet if it is true that nature itself is something presupposed on the part of spirit, it is still spirit itself that posits this dimension of its own self-externality, so that spirit remains "absolute power" precisely because it can freely release itself (*sich entlassen*) "in the shape of independent diversity, necessity, contingency, caprice, and opinion in all their externality."[20] In short, this total remainder of spirit is, at bottom, all that has been rejected or cast away from the ultimate summit of the absolute Idea, in relation to which, as Hegel says, "Everything else [*Alles Übrige*] is error, obscurity, struggle, caprice, and transience [*Vergänglichkeit*]."[21] It is just that this remnant, regarded in distributive terms, is also the sum total (*Allheit*) of all the beings that exist, for every being or entity affirms itself—in pride and vanity—as something independent and possessed of an absolute significance on its own account. Here, then, we are confronted with a freedom that is de-ranged (strictly speaking: as something that is outside or "beside itself" precisely because it creates externality or exteriority itself and sees the latter as at once alien and necessary—in the sense of the Greek *anankē*).

We should clearly understand that what is so disturbing and disconcerting here is not just that there are natural pluralities and manifolds, divergences and marginalities that elude the grasp of the concept. For in the end it would prove as tedious as it is futile to attempt to provide some exhaustive classification of anything and everything that populates or constitutes the universe as a whole.[22]

No, the truly disturbing thing is that this gratuitousness of being, this persisting challenge to the principle of sufficient reason, springs from the dimension of spirit that Hegel specifically characterizes as "free," albeit in the vulgar sense of "arbitrary" (he expressly recognizes that we are talking about "arbitrary occurrences of spirit with respect to its representations"[23]) rather than in the authentically Hegelian sense of Being-with-Itself-in-the-Other, for here the spirit is no longer present, neither with Itself (rather, it cannot properly conceive of itself here), nor in the Other. On the contrary, "It" (*Es, id*) is "outside" or "beside" itself; it is not even the Other of Itself, but the absolutely Other, that which escapes the play of *aliquid / aliud*, and is thus neither nature nor spirit: it is not conceivable as *alter*.

3. The Strange Heart of Reason

There is a mystery or enigma here that speculative reason is powerless to unveil: what hinders the complete identification of Spirit and the Idea (despite the fact that both are qualified as "absolute") is rooted in this internal position of the irrational as a kind of frayed or fractured exteriority. And here it is imperative to proceed with some care and precision: it is not simply that the Idea cannot be identified with Spirit because the latter, that which is most concrete of all, adds a "plus" or surplus (the natural power of free choice), and it is just this plus from which we abstract in order to arrive at the "pure logical essentialities." It alone guarantees the ongoing progress of society and the sciences: the task of recognition is known precisely as this task, although it is by no means fully accomplished for all that.[24] Rather, what it is important to underline above all is this: neither is the Idea absolutely transparent to itself (on the contrary, in its ultimate core it is atomic and impenetrable with regard to itself[25]), nor indeed can Spirit recognize itself fully in its world. Or we could say, if we wish, with an exactness that reverts to paradox, that it recognizes itself absolutely in a position of recusal, of arbitrary refusal against knowledge.

It is not that reason unveils a mystery (which until now it had itself remained), but that the Mystery breaks out in the heart of reason itself. What is uncanny here, in short, is not that nature is a "Bacchic God" that is incapable of holding back or restraining itself, that is incapable of self-possession, for that is indeed the definition of nature, the *logos* of the illogical. The uncanny thing is that "in nature the unity of the concept is hidden,"[26] and that this occultation or concealment, before all time and reason, can never be recuperated. There is no *Aufhebung* or "sublation" of this hiddenness (or better, to express this in the medium of religious representation), there is no *Second Coming* in Hegel; there is no end of the world, and hence no ultimate redemption through grace nor any final righteous condemnation.

This untamable and inhospitable latency or potency that marks and darkens the heart of the Hegelian system is also what effectively explains something that is hardly compatible with what we might call "official Hegelianism," with the usual chatter about the "emperor of thought" who would finally "close all the circles," etc., etc. I am talking about something expressly acknowledged by Hegel, namely that true religious consciousness finds its proper place not in religion but in philosophy. Speaking in strictly "noological" terms (i.e., speaking at the level of the philosophy of subjective spirit), Hegel distinguishes three stages within the Kingdom of Spirit: "the first estate [*Stand*] is that of immediate, naive religion and of faith; the second is that of the understanding, the estate of the so-called cultures, of reflection and Enlightenment; and finally the third estate is the community of philosophy." It is with these words that Hegel concluded his second lecture course on the philosophy of religion in 1824.[27] And he repeats the same things even more concisely at the very end of the third series of lectures he delivered in 1827.[28] Thus, we see here how Hegel simply describes the "third estate" as "the rational cognition of religion." We should clearly recognize how in a kind of threefold fashion—from a noological, historical, and even sociological perspective—the place of religion tout court, the place of the absolute or consummate religion, the religion that is adequate to its own concept, appears to start disappearing in favor of philosophy itself (a philosophy that would prove to be just as ungrateful, to take up Hegel's own comparison, as the act of eating that consumes the material of nourishment that prompts and gives meaning to the act in the first place[29]).

In effect, the first two stages or "estates" are intrinsically inadequate and have ended in failure. The first of these (which Hegel himself had once defended, in a modified form, under the name of *Volksreligion* or a "religion of the people") is based entirely on the heart and on human feelings, that is, on "the subject so far as the various practical feelings are in it all combined."[30] The heart is a subjective response here, is the memory and interiorized form of the "fear of the Lord." It is indeed, on the human side, the beginning of all wisdom. For, in the first place, it is in the heart that human beings behold their inner determinations (their destiny) as their own immanent cause or concern, rather than as something that is externally imposed on them. And in the second place, confronted by the abstract demands of the understanding, the unification and combination of feelings here does, in a certain way, capture the real world in its entirety. The domain of the heart colors things with an affective dimension and transforms or meta-phorizes them in a way that allows them to resonate with us and allows us to relate to the world as a whole. Yet the heart itself, on its own, belongs to each of us individually, and it can also prove resistant to communication and community, refractory to reason and society.

More familiar perhaps are the serious failures that Hegel associates with the second stage we have mentioned: the stage of "reflection" at the level of the abstract understanding, and indeed also that of Fideism as the inner antagonist of the understanding. This is an antagonism (like that between Fichte and Jacobi, for example) that nonetheless ends up leading to the same thing, according to Hegel, as we can clearly see from his remarks in the opening *Lectures on the Proofs of the Existence of God* and in the concluding paragraphs of the section that is entitled "The Preliminary Concept" in the so-called *Lesser Logic* of the *Encyclopaedia*. For we are confronted here with the same empty and abstract identity of the "Supreme Being" of the Enlightenment (or as the German literally expresses it: *das Höchste Wesen*, the highest or ultimate Essence). We have here the same movement, the movement of reflection, that is equally fixed or fixated, as we might say, in contrary directions: between an initial extreme (the point of abstract intuition: the form of immediate knowing that stubbornly refuses to move beyond this starting point and fails to acknowledge that as yet it has actually captured nothing at all) and its own subsequent product (the final point of abstract thought: the form of purely reflective metaphysics that cannot actually think anything once it has quantified and arrested every conceptual determination). We are left, then, with nothing but the insipid—and nihilistic—repetition of the Identical, with mere repetition itself: "abstract identity as the principle and criterion of truth."[31]

It is the third "estate" alone, according to Hegel, that can attain the unity-in-difference of the spirit and the community, of form and content, of logical universality and ontic fullness. And this estate—because it comprehends religion in a truly rational way, and indeed only because it does so—is the community of philosophy. It is important, in effect, to insist from the beginning that the sphere in which spirit recognizes itself, the sphere of absolute spirit, is—as Hegel explicitly says—the sphere of religion,[32] and not that of philosophy, for the latter does not itself constitute any such specific sphere or domain, being nothing but the "liminal" and thus ambiguous movement (at once closing and opening) of the intersection and overlapping of spheres. Thus, Hegel writes: "Religion in general is the ultimate and supreme sphere of human consciousness, whether as feeling, will, representation, knowing, or cognition—the absolute result, that region into which the human being passes over [*übergeht*] as the region of absolute truth" (*V-Rel.* 3, 79; Hodgson 1, 170).

Religion is, then, the region of truth. Philosophy, on the other hand, is the activity through which human beings advance toward and raise themselves to that which, in infinitely overcoming their riven naturalness, constitutes in turn their own most intimate substance. The human being cannot calmly dwell in philosophy, for philosophy provides no stay or resting place; on the contrary, it is nothing but movement, fearlessly open to the elements, exposed to the inhospitable. It is quite true that in the sphere of religion we find that form and content coincide with one another absolutely, and that this coincidence constitutes the ultimate speculative foundation. But human consciousness itself, in spite of attaining its supreme state of being (*Zustand*) in this sphere (cf. *V-Rel.* 5, 3), cannot simply overcome that split or scission (between certainty and truth, between the objective and the subjective) that, precisely, constitutes it as such. This is the region in which it dwells. Yet the rift that marks this region, the furrow that also makes it a *borderline*, does not exist or stand out as such, for it is nothing but scission: that *scission-or-consciousness* that enters, in the sphere of religion, into paroxysm.

4. "I Am the Unity of Fire and Water"

It is here that strife or conflict springs forth. I am not placed (through my sins, let us say, or through original sin itself) into this field of battle (*in hac lacrimarum valle*). No. *Ich bin der Kampf selbst*, I am this very struggle. I am the unity (not the unification or combination) of fire and water (of the *praxis* that consumes itself in that which it itself consumes, of the *theoria* that extends its gaze to everything, turning this into something vain and empty in a kind of liquefaction of the flesh). And, once again, we must fully recognize the irreducibility of the extremes involved here. Hegel claims that I am (and indivisibly so, for it is the "I" that is in question) the "very point where what is now (*bald*) separated and divided touches that which is now (*bald*) reconciled and united" (*V-Rel.* 3, 121; Hodgson 1, 213).

There is a tragic aspect here that the Greek soul could not know of, or indeed even suspect. The Christian human being (modern man tout court) is unable to reconcile his empirical present with his intelligible past. He *feels* that he is this connection-and-separation of different tenses. And on this internal strife or conflict (*Widerstreit*) of mutually opposed moments he bestows the name of "I." He feels, and also thinks, and also acts. He is the conjugation, the holding and yoking together, of the extremes in this process (Hegel himself speaks of a *Zusammenhalten* and a *Zusammengebundensein* here). But this con-jugation lives solely in what is con-jugated, in this process of con-joining, without therefore being simply and entirely "for itself." The relation that the "I" itself is cannot be self-referential in character. It cannot escape this struggle, as it does in the famous struggle of consciousness and self-consciousness (the dialectic of master and slave), where one of the contending parties surrenders to the other through the fear of death, the absolute Lord and Master. No. For now self-consciousness is regarded from the perspective of spirit itself. And here, both extremes must founder and come to grief, enduring the real and logical trial, in every single case, of death.

The absolute Lord and Master, will this perhaps be the appearance (*Ercheinung*) of absolute Love? Yes, of course it will. But the question is, what is it that actually comes to be loved here? One loves what one loses. Once he is dead, God cannot die again. In his place, and through him, everything perishes. God loves this transient and fugitive character of things, for which he himself has arrived too late. For which he, the essence-that-has-already-been (*gewesen*), has already passed away entirely; he is on his turn that, what is entirely past (*vergangen ist*).

In this regard, Karl Rosenkranz has preserved some significant observations of Hegel's, which he dated to the Nuremberg period when Hegel prepared the teaching materials collected in the *Philosophical Propaedeutic*,[33] although we now know they were actually written in the Berlin period (1821). In this summary text, Hegel presents three important aspects of what he took to be the essence of Christianity. First, the Resurrection and Ascension of Christ have a proper meaning only in the sphere of faith (*nur für den Glauben*). Second, in the Lutheran Protestantism that for Hegel was the religion in which Christianity comes most truly to be understood, "the priests are only teachers." And thirdly—and this is the aspect I should like to emphasize most strongly—God's reconciliation with Man is something that has already happened (*geschehen*) in and for itself, and redemption therefore lies in our conscious acceptance of common or "ordinary actuality" (*die gemeine Wirklichkeit*), in the hallowing of that which is most lowly (*Niedrigkeit*), but that is no longer despised as such.

In fact, Christianity stands revealed as a "return to life," that is, as the legitimation and comprehension of *Sittlichkeit*, of the "ethical life" of the people, the world of family, society, and the state. Since this reconciliation between the realms of politics and religion, of *Gesellschaft* and *Gemeinde*, has in principle already happened (and can only therefore be known by internal reflection on its own narrative, that is, from within the enactment of the *récit*), it is this "essential" past that grounds History (*Geschichte*) and gives meaning to the common and shared life of human beings both within and against nature. This is the spirit of Christianity for Hegel. But this same spirit needs to show the figure of Jesus of Nazareth as broken *terminus medius* between God and human beings, as subject to the harsh law of the apodictic judgment presented in the *Science of Logic*, a law that destines all effective reality to perish, incapable as it is of sustaining the living fission between its concept and its existence (see *WdL* (*GW* 12, 88). Jesus is the paradigmatic figure for this innermost rupture, divided as he is between Father/Heaven and Mother/Earth. Only if Christ dies for us and through us, only if he is transfigured into the Crucified Christ, can we understand him as the inversion of Adam, that is, as the "perfect return" to the Origin that turns him into the Redeemer. Paraphrasing Saint Paul against the letter of his doctrine, but perhaps even capturing its *spirit*, I would dare to say that if Christ be not dead, if he does not remain dead and is thus transfigured into the Spirit of the community, then our faith is in vain (I Corinthians, ch. 15, v. 14).

That living fission, that contradiction between Law and the Natural Man, between universality and carnal singularity, must disappear from the real external world in order to bestow life and meaning on man's innermost being, even if this would in the end consume the body of man through the fire that burns in every human heart. This is the effect that religion produces on the natural side of man: *dem Natürlichen abzusterben*, to allow all considerations for natural things to die.[34]

The essence of the human being, the authentic consciousness of finite spirit, lies precisely in this movement of cutting and separating, for it is a pure *limen*, a de-marcation of things, an incision in the real: *diese Negativität und Abscheidung ist es, die mein Wesen konstituiert*.[35] Noli me tangere. The hand with which the risen Christ refuses the tender approaches of Mary Magdalene in the immortal painting of Correggio perfectly catches and expresses the "integrity" of Christ here. All of him is captured in this hand that refuses, and in this refusal, simultaneously withdraws. This is not the hand of a living being, but neither is it the hand of a cadaver. It is the hand (at once limit and delimitation, a borderline of transgression and recognition) of a certain *oc-cision* (a cutting off or cutting down), of one suspended at the utter limit: in himself, he is indeed, was indeed, God, for death is now his past. But as long as he has not yet been transfigured into the spirit and transfigured as the spirit of the community (figuratively speaking in terms of pictorial religious representation: as long as he has not yet "ascended into heaven"), he continues to appear as nothing more than man: this immediate sensuous subject. It is futile to ask whether he could have been touched by the all-too-carnal hand of Mary Magdalene. This would be like asking whether, apart from this gesture of refusal, Christ would continue to be a man or would already have returned to being God. But the integrity, the perfect wholeness, of Christ consists in and exhausts itself in this very gesture. "Man" and "God" are nothing but two extremes here, and as such nothing but unilateral abstractions. Ultimately speaking, these extremes come forth solely from the limit, from the benevolent *Mitte*.

Here, and only here, in this belated and evanescent Christ, who is at once ceasing to be and coming into being, in this pure *Werden des Wesens*, is it really possible to speak of a true *imitatio Christi* on the part of the Christian human being. I am this hand that refuses: "The essential moment of this separation or *oc-cisionality* (*Abgeschiedenheit*) of spirit consists in the way that I can abstract from everything that is immediate and external. This occisionality is withdrawn (*entnommen*) from temporality etc." (*V-Rel.* 3, 104f.; Hodgson 1, 196). I have chosen this admittedly strange term "occisionality" (derived from the Latin *occido*—compare "the Occident") to capture, as far as this is possible in a language indebted to Latin, something of the strangeness of the original German word *Abgeschiedenheit*.[36] Taken literally, the word suggests the state or process of being "cut off." In the context of everyday language *ein Abgeschiedener* is a "dead person," and *abscheiden* simply means to die or "pass on." (And in Spanish legal language the word *occiso* is still used for the "deceased"). But the evocative force of the German word is even stronger. A literal interpretation of these passages from Hegel would undoubtedly appear somewhat negative or nihilistic in character. In that case we should then have to say that the philosophical "translation" of the representational religious language of the immortality of the soul is simply the mortality of man, and the ephemerality in general of everything that exists. And instead of talking about two interwoven and interpenetrating regions (time and eternity, God and the world), there would only be in truth a single ephemeral and ever-perishing one. And any other conception would simply be a fabrication or invention on the part of . . . (and we may fill this in with whatever is ideologically required in each case, from infamous priests to people's commissars).

But Hegel is not remotely interested in such banal conceptions, however "correct" they may seem to common sense. The truth is, rather, that the death of Jesus Christ in the context of natural cyclical time is the beginning of historical human time. While Jesus was alive it was absolutely necessary that those closest to him did not recognize who he really was. And would it, indeed, be too outrageous to say that he himself did not recognize what he was either, and this is ultimately the reason why his terrible outcry to the Father who had abandoned him sounds so natural to us? Why did the Father abandon him if not that the Scriptures might be fulfilled? Not indeed the Writings of the Old Testament, but the ones not yet written, those of the future that were written in the blood of an innocent victim who, it may be, did not even know what was being done to him. And in fact no Saint Paul or Saint Luke was there to bestow a retroactive meaning on something that they neither saw nor touched. It was something in which they could only believe.

5. Natural Death and the Death of Death

It is worth pondering the fact that Jesus of Nazareth did not leave any traces that we could properly describe as features of *Sittlichkeit*, of the ethical sphere of the community. This "second nature" is typically displayed in the context of human relationships. Yet the Gospels contain hardly any allusions to the relationship between the son and his purported father, the carpenter. Jesus turned away from his brothers and his mother toward the formless and ungrateful masses that he himself had rejected not so long before. And the sublimated encounter with Mary Magdalene takes place solely as a preparation for his own death, and one that destroys the root of all carnal desire. And finally, the relationship with his disciples could hardly be worse: they fight among themselves over the place that awaits them in the Kingdom of Heaven. The disciples themselves will be transformed only after the death of Jesus, and only by suffering a martyr's death. They will turn into Apostles in the same way as the promised Messiah turned into Christ, who will return as the Holy Spirit. It is evident that the Gospels, the Pauline Epistles, and the whole of the New Testament have been built up from and on behalf of the Cross, and only after it. A Cross of Glory that reveals (since "glory" is a word equivalent to the Greek *doxa* or "appearance") that Christ is no longer with us. Before he suffered crucifixion he might indeed have been the promised Messiah, but manifestly not as the Crucified One. The latter appears solely as disappearance, as an essentially evanescent quality. In mathematical terms the Crucified One is a passage toward the uttermost limit. Pontius Pilate, the reasonable Roman, and thus a sceptical and tolerant kind of man, attempted to speak to this prisoner, whom he saw as an exalted *prophet* and a visionary, although Pilate did not exercise all of the power he possessed in opposition to the Sanhedrin, with which he needed to coexist and maintain diplomatic relations. He does not realize that Christ is a pure negation of any dialogue. For He, the founder of all communities that regard themselves as universal, as truly *catholic*, only exists by banishing himself from men and Gods. Christ has a meaning solely after his death, and only in this way does he confer a meaning on everything. Only in this way can he be remembered and ritually celebrated. Who would dare to say that it was Jesus of Nazareth, the son of Mary and Joseph, who had been resurrected? Or have we forgotten the story of Emmaus? It is the return of the Son to the Father who has resurrected him, and it is at the same time the self-fulfillment of the father in the son. It is the spirit that is resurrected, and not the Son of Man whose lifeless head rests on Mary Magdalene's golden hair. If so, then with his death he has redeemed us from a merely natural death, thus opening up the path to our own sacrificial death, or what Hegel calls "the death of death" (*V-Rel.* 5, 67f.; Hodgson 3, 131f.).

If natural death is the wearing away of singularity, and at the same time the return to the Mother as putrefaction and decomposition, to the abstract universality that corresponds to all that is natural, then the "death of death," the redemption afforded by Christ's sacrifice, must revert back to and negatively strengthen the natural relation through which universality is preserved almost as a solvent medium. And that is accomplished thanks to the constant liquefaction of singularities. The domain of legal organization (the structure of people's rights and responsibilities), the organization of the family (the institution of marriage), and the political domain (the realm of obedience to law) are symbolically united through the *Aufhebung* of religion in the ethical life of the community: this would be the aforementioned "return to life" that is accomplished through the Holy Spirit. This is that transformation of the old "Catholic" vows of chastity, poverty, and obedience that is accomplished throughout modern religion and, according to Hegel, specifically in Lutheranism. Each individual displays himself in the community—the existence of which is constituted through the free and self-conscious citizens in the life of the state—and the service to the community consists, for Hegel, in allowing all of our immediate desires with regard to natural things to die. When the individual thus gives himself selflessly to "second nature," he loses that abstract universality, his *Gattungswesen*, which bound him and overcomes his own singularity within the institutions that he serves. (See *V-Rel.* 5, 152; Hodgson 3, 221f.).

This is a triumph of the artificial, of what is made, over nature as what is given, the triumph of the Christian *citoyen* over the *animal rationale*. But what is the difference between this second nature, which ethically demands self-sacrifice, and first nature, which *naturally* demands the death of the animal? It is the very same difference that we discover between concrete universality and abstract universality. The ethical sphere lives out of self-determination, that is, it lives out of that freedom of its members that constitutes its existence (its *Existenz*, and no more its mere *Dasein*), in order to overcome its own limitations and rise to its very *concept*, to its ought-to-be, by denying its own abstract base, its own to-be.

What remains as the perennial result of this sacrifice is the gesture, the word, the act—all these continue to influence the symbolic network of interactions that are sustained through the negative *determination* of nature. All that is left is that which opens the future and allows the unforeseen and unexpected to arise. And in each particular case (as family member, as economic agent, as citizen) the process of self-abnegation opens up very complex paths, along with different degrees of freedom in the *Sittlichkeit* that belongs to the realm of objective spirit, because this self-abnegation presupposes a total sacrifice, a pure negation of nature.

This pure negation rejects—and condenses within this rejection—every merely habitual feature, refuses the uniformity and monotony of natural life. It rejects the total condensation of that inertia that we call death (natural and abstract death). This rejection (according to the demands of the ethical realm) specifically denies natural death as such. And, like the Passion of Christ, it may therefore be described as the *death of death*.

This is the reason why Christ died on the cross, died an infamous death that expelled him from the domain of Roman legality, that same legality that was to make every man equal to every other man on the sole condition that there would no longer be any "world," but only that arid and monotonous relationship between the various districts and provinces under a single legal authority, and an arbitrary authority at that. The death of Christ transpired not because he could "no longer bear to live," and not because he was unable "to accustom himself" to the life around him. On the contrary, all the ephemeral pleasures of this life were excluded for him. There was perhaps only one he could enjoy: the balsam with which he was anointed by Mary the sister of Lazarus in preparation for his death.

In this sense Incarnation, or *Menschwerdung*, does not signify the salvation but the condemnation of the earth. According to Hegel, *the divinization of man involves the desecration of nature*, for the human being is the turning point where nature finds itself inflected or inverted. This is the strange being that emerges, returns from his origin, and turns against that very origin: a rootless or deracinated being, an "ecumenical" being who can inhabit the whole of the earth and yet is everywhere de trop, everywhere an outcast. Here we find nature renouncing itself, death turning its sting against itself. The condemnation of nature is consummated in the death of Christ (one that is antinatural in its full sense). Hegel does not really speak about the resurrection of Christ—as we have seen, he relegates this "representation" to the sphere of faith—because this death, like every good *limes* or boundary, is a double-edged one. In terms of our natural origin it utters the truth of nature, that is, that nature is the *Idea's own past* (cf. *V-Rel.* 5, 28; Hodgson 3, 90–91). In the context of this empirical past, of this essential pastness or *Gewesenweit*, which is responsible for the eventual decay and decomposition of every human being, the Christian believer can never be reconciled with his own body and corporeal sensibility. But in the context of our spiritual calling, this same death is already the resurrection of perennial life. And its truth therefore lies in the fact that it is precisely *spirit's future*. Hence this double-edged death is also the condition of the possibility of history. Without death, without all of us being already dead in Christ (if it is indeed true that *Einmal is Allemal*),[37] there would be no universal history, nor would there be a world *qua saeculum* (for *kosmos* is not the same as "this Age"). Death is the "essential past" of human beings, and thus opens up the possibility of meaningful existence, for here human action is oriented from the perspective of a finitude that accepts and shares meaning. The *true infinite*, as Hegel calls it, dwells in death, and thus neither in "this life" nor in the "next life" beyond this one. The limit has no limit. What the Cross reveals is the Absolute. From this point of view the well-known words of the Apostle: "For me to live is Christ, and to die is gain," rings like a tragic utterance.

What the human being calls death, every death (*Einmal ist Allemal*) is really the *Vollendung*, the accomplishment of death in and as everyday life, the consummation of this movement that is unaware of its own end—as at once conclusion and final purpose. This death is, from the beginning, the ground zero of existence, the ground on which this Great Theater of the World is staged, like the bones that are the irreducible remains that this agile and supple death cannot assimilate just because they are so fixed and rigid in death. "They are the design on which the body of man is carved." It would be easy to explain these words by Don Francisco de Quevedo simply by ascribing them to the radical pessimism of this poet, to his Stoic outlook and his disenchantment with a decadent Spanish culture, and so on. It is quite true that all elements are there, and especially evident in a moral satire such as *The Dreams*. And it is also true that speculative thought is the *quinta essentia*, the reflective focus that can explain the sense and moral of the story. But this does not imply some empty form of reductionism. The great Baroque Spanish poet is closer to Hegel in indicating that death is not a future *event* that we would have to face (by means of "reflection," according to Martin Luther, or by a kind of "imitation" or anticipation, according to Ignatius of Loyola), but rather the purposeless movement of existence as such, thus reducing it to a mere dream. Death, which taken by itself was regarded as true and tangible reality, turns out to be "a dream image with its face to the past." Like Psyche drinking from the waters of Oblivion, as Hegel says, giving a Christian and Dantean turn to this image rather than employing a Platonic or Virgilian one (*V-Rel.* 3, 5, 32, and 62; Hodgson 1, 75, 114, and 150), the soul that is immersed in the waters of the consummate religion sees how all the concerns of life are reflected and broken up in ephemeral appearance, as *Schein. The soul lives as if it were already dead.* This is how Hegel inverts the common attitude of consciousness. We must live mortally as if natural death would never take place. And this would be the only possible death of death. Once more, and again obsessively, I am to let the natural be extinguished within myself: *Absterben dem Natürlichen.*

This also explains the apparent paradox according to which the fulfillment of the death of Christ, once grasped at the level of the concept, serves to open up world history. As in Quevedo's poem, where the bones are the ground or canvas, as it were, on which the human body is projected and developed, so for Hegel the Cross of Christ contains *die ganze Geschichte*, the whole of history (cf. *V-Rel.* 5, 85; Hodgson 3, 149–50). This is the Aleph where everything comes together: the chiasmus of the Universe, the refulgent ground zero of time. This is not an event that belongs to one particular period of time, for this *Ereignis*, as we may say in German, is *epochemachend* or epoch-making, the *epochē* that makes all epochs possible. It is the character of time as natural time, the naturalness of time, which dies, with its monotonous, repetitive, and vacuous character. And this is why the time of Christ's Advent signifies the plenitude or fulfillment of time (*die erfüllte Zeit*).

But if it is true now that the time is fulfilled, replete with *logos*, with *Verbum*; if it is true, expressed in the language of religious representation, that the Father has abased himself to the level of the Son, and dies with him (for it is God himself, and not merely Jesus of Nazareth, that dies; see *V-Rel.* 5, 60; Hodgson 3, 125); and if it is true that the Son is incarnated in the human being as such, then eternity is already in time, bestowing meaning and direction on time. Heaven descends, and is transplanted to earth, while earth rises and is concentrated in the Cross on Mount Golgotha (we remember the earthquake and the graves that open at the hour of his death). But if there is no return to the Father, there is nothing left but the world. What faith calls "the resurrection" is what we, the philosophers, behold and understand as the *Aufhebung* or "sublation" of Christ as the "essential past" of man. What remains with us until the end of time (or shall we say, until time is consummated, until we are all consummated?) is the Spirit of and in the Community. Christ becomes a kind of atmosphere here. For what Hegel celebrates is neither the Resurrection nor the Ascension, but Pentecost (Whitsun): the Advent of the *Paraclete* as universal fire and flame, that is to say, the gift of speaking every language, which is the foundation of society, and specifically of Christian society—the only place where the individual as a singular being properly dwells. The only place where everything is redeemed, and is restituted in and through its own negation.

But then we who read and meditate with Hegel no longer need to prepare ourselves for dying, no longer need to practice the spiritual exercises of imitating or anticipating death. Those who walk with Hegel can be neither Lutherans nor Jesuits. For Hegel death is neither a terrible nor a banal event. Hegel understood death as the base or canvass on which the body of the universe is carved. To think is to be dead, understood as a determinate negation—as the negation of the negation—or as the death of death. In this sense death is something *logical*. In and during our life we die abstractly as the mere immediate negation of a Death that secretly drives us onward: this is *natural*. In any case, it is true that we, as philosophers, still live in a community of believers, of the faithful, and continue to exist as immediate sense-consciousness. But precisely because we are aware of this, we are estranged from ourselves, as we consider both consciousness and the community. We thus realize that we have been evicted from both life and death, without adequately stepping either into life, that is, into sense-consciousness, or into death as it is accepted and acknowledged in the community of the faithful. And we remain at the threshold between both of these spheres, petrified, longing for something that cannot come.

Chapter III

Death Is a Gulp of Water

(*La Terreur* in World History)

1. Hegel and the Revolution—After Marxism

If I may invoke the title of a once-celebrated book that is now perhaps (unjustly as I believe) almost forgotten, namely *Reason and Revolution*, it seems imperative for us—today, above all, given the political problems and crises that beset the failing states of southern Europe and the possibly imminent shipwreck of the European Union itself—to look once again at Hegel's view of the French Revolution in general and, more particularly, at the *conceptual* interpretation of the latter that he provided in the *Phenomenology of Spirit*. We need to do this, in the first place, to recognize the merely historical or largely obsolete character of the literature that was essentially inspired by Marx and in which—with a few exceptions—Hegel the philosopher was valued principally as a precursor, albeit an idealist one, of Marx and of *his* conception of dialectical method. And this despite the fact that the perspective in question proved generally sympathetic to Hegel, resulting sometimes—within the *warm* range of Marxism—in a rather exalted level of praise that was hardly envisioned by the defenders of Soviet orthodoxy, anxious or jealous perhaps lest the "dead dog" with whom Marx had deigned to "coquette" (as he put it in the postface to the second edition of

Capital) might actually end up casting a shadow over the founder of so-called *scientific socialism*.

Among the representatives of what I have described as the warmer range of commentators I would merely single out the three notable and well-known examples of Lukács, Bloch, and Marcuse.[1] From the side of the supposedly orthodox doctrine of dialectical materialism, on the other hand, the most deluded testimony is perhaps that of Joseph Stalin, who in 1944, at the height of World War II, saw fit to denigrate Hegel in the closing session of the Central Committee of the Communist Party of the Soviet Union. The Georgian "philosopher" accused the philosopher of Stuttgart of using his writings to encourage the growth of German nationalism and of chauvinism in general, thus effectively transforming Hegel from a precursor of Marx into a promoter of fascism. This at least with respect to the consequences of his thought. In itself the supposed philosophy of Hegel was simply interpreted in terms of the aristocratic reaction to the French Revolution.

This devastating assessment, as we could only expect, would soon make its influence felt in the *Great Soviet Encyclopaedia*, which was presented by the editors in their introduction to the German edition as "the most comprehensive [*umfassendste*] scientific work produced in the history of humanity." If the *Encyclopaedia* is to be believed (along with Stalin), then not only Hegel but also Kant, Fichte, and Schelling had essentially unleashed a "struggle against materialism" (*Kampf gegen den Materialismus*). It is claimed in general that "German Idealism took its fundamental task to be that of combating the theory and praxis of the bourgeois French Revolution." Yet it is supposed to be Hegel in particular, the "objective idealist" (*der objective Idealist*), who specifically "defended the interests of the Junker class and of the bourgeoisie, mystified the historical process and converted the history of human society into a pure history of thought. [. . .] He idealized the Prussian monarchy, intervened in favour of unjust wars, and attempted at all costs to denigrate the Slavs."[2]

I hardly think it is necessary to challenge such foolish claims as these. The only thing of interest here, it seems to me, is to identify the inspiration behind an *Encyclopaedia* that claims in its pages to capture nothing less than the various transformations and intellectual achievements of Humanity in its entirety, even as the work proclaims itself the bearer, indeed the very guide and light, of a genuinely *internationalist* mode of thought, whereas in truth it allows us to glimpse a miserable chauvinism that is evidently greater than that which it purports to criticize in Hegel. With regard to the alleged denigration or degradation (*Herabsetzung*) "at all costs" of the Slavic peoples on the part of the German philosopher what we actually find in his work are remarks such as these: "The third region [i.e., with respect to the relation between history and geography in the context of Europe—F.D.] is the north-east of Europe. It contains the northern plains, which have a peculiar character of their own; they once belonged to the Slavonic nations, and form a link with Asia, particularly with Russia and Poland. These countries are late arrivals in the series of historical states, and they maintain a constant connection with Asia."[3] These surely appear to be incontrovertible observations, unless of course we wished to turn history into a "pure history of thought," and an *ideological* one at that, or unless Soviet Russia perhaps regarded its own Asiatic component as rather degrading. It is quite true that, a little further on, when he speaks of the "great Slavic nation," Hegel claims that it constitutes an "intermediate nationality" between the European and the Asian spirit. And he continues: "Yet this entire body of peoples has not yet entered, as an independent element, into the series of forms which reason has assumed in the world. Whether it will do so in the future is a question that does not concern us; for in history we have to do with the past" (*Phil. Hist.*; Sibree, 363; translation adapted). Now an intelligent chauvinism, so to speak, might well reverse this evaluation, and with good reason. For it would be able to argue, in the spirit of Hegel, that if not then yet in the twentieth century Russia has indeed burst upon the field of "universal history" (and to what effect!) with the October Revolution, and might even boast of assuming (for seventy-five years at least) the role of the World Spirit. And certainly Hegel himself allowed us to entertain this possibility since he expressly says that this mass of peoples "has not *yet* entered" the field of World History. But let us finally leave these foolish reflections to their fate (and fortunately enough they are also innocuous ones above all with respect to the political and ideological exploitation of philosophy, and in view of a new Terror—now already passed—that on that occasion seemed to have nothing to do with that freedom[4] whose absolute expansion, according to Hegel, would usher in the French Revolution).

2. Living and Thinking One's Own Time

But if we wish to question Hegel, today, in this regard (or, rather, if we are to allow Hegel's words to put our own epoch into question), this is because it is only recently (as if hardly twenty-five years have passed) that the meaning of history appears to have abandoned the *teleological* ideal of revolution (which from the beginning, and in principle, could only be a worldwide one), and opened itself up, perhaps catastrophically, to the "viral infection" of terrorism within a process of globalization that is not only economic in character, but also cultural and political in its overall tendency. In effect, until the fall of the sadly famous Berlin Wall in 1989 (and shortly afterward of so-called "real existing socialism" in the Soviet Union and its satellite states in 1991), the precisely two hundred years that separate these events from the outbreak of the French Revolution had essentially been regarded—whether in hope or in fear—as the Age of Revolutions, with its long string of outbreaks (1789, 1830, 1848, 1917, 1959 (in Cuba), and up until, on a generous reading at least, 1968, the "revolutionary" year of my own youth). It was only logical, in this connection, to ask ourselves about the attitude that Hegel adopted in the face of revolution when it comes to understanding a thinker who more than fulfilled the two sayings that he himself bequeathed to us regarding the task of *living* and of *thinking* one's own time.

The first saying is this: "As far as the individual is concerned, each one of us is a son of his own time."[5] Now the time of the individual Hegel himself is marked by a chain of revolutions: the first "revolution" (let us be generous here too, and follow the account already proposed by Hannah Arendt[6]) would be the revolt of the North American colonies against the British (1776); the great Revolution erupted when Hegel was an eighteen-year-old student in the Tübingen seminary; and a year before his death he was anxiously following the events of the brief and decisive "July Revolution" of 1830 in France,[7] and was also rather disturbed at the imminent prospect of the Great Reform Bill passing into English law (indeed his very last publication was dedicated to this subject). For Hegel specifically feared that the forces then in play "would lead not to reform but to revolution."[8] In this regard, among all the major thinkers of the epoch, only Schelling appears to have been even *more* a son of his revolutionary time than Hegel, given that the former lived to witness, at the very doors of his house in Berlin, the revolution of 1848.

The second saying contains a famous definition and follows directly from the first one: "thus philosophy too is *its own time comprehended in thoughts*" (*Rechtsphil.*, 27; Knox, 15). Now it would hardly be an exaggeration to say that Hegel spent his entire life trying to comprehend the French Revolution and its consequences, that is, to raise it to the highest possible level of conceptual articulation. Thus it is as if we were dealing with a kind of undesirable triad here, for the life of Hegel, as we have said, was effectively framed by the first great revolutionary upheaval (1789), a product of Enlightenment philosophy; by the antithetical reaction to that event, as if one could revert to the *Ancien Régime* (the Restoration from 1815); and lastly by a new revolution in which bourgeois liberalism would establish itself in France (the *Révolution de juillet* of 1830), immediately followed by the important electoral reform in Britain (1831). As far as Germany itself was concerned, in the period from around 1820 the majority of states saw the establishment of openly reactionary regimes, actively involved in suppressing or delaying the introduction of political constitutions, imposing an iron rule of censorship and stubbornly persecuting or expelling *awkward* academics from their chairs: the "usual suspects" (it was not for nothing that the process unleashed by the Carlsbad Decrees was described as *die Demagogenverfolgung*: "the persecution of the demagogues").[9] Not a trace, now, of what was desired or anticipated in 1806, namely the idea that the relative political failure of the French Revolution (*la Terreur*) might have worked as a *pharmakon* in the old European world, ultimately resulting in the reorganization and revitalization of the "spiritual masses" (as Hegel calls them in the *Phenomenology*) that had formerly been violently repressed (a possible allusion to the republican and then Napoleonic reorganization of the former regimes that were then established as new states, such as the Helvetian or the Cisapline Republics, or were transformed into constitutional monarchies, such as, for example, the Spain of José I). Karl Rosenkranz, in his important biography of Hegel, bears witness to these things, to this hoped-for renewal of a Europe that would be capable of bringing its particular usages, customs, and traditions into harmony with a free acknowledgement of universal reason: all free spirits during this period, he tells us, "united in the ardent expectation of an ethical rebirth of Europe once the Rights of Humanity had been decreed."[10] Even more clearly than from the words of Rosenkranz, we may gather as much from what the *Phenomenology of Spirit* openly declares, namely that on a much broader and more comprehensive, and indeed strictly philosophical, level, the Spirit has now passed over to Germany, first assuming an essentially interior form in the sphere of *Moralität* before emerging at last into the light in a society religiously transformed as the community or *Gemeinde*, thus sealing the reconciliation of the individual consciences that stand confronting one another in the final shape of the "forgiveness of sins."[11]

All of these things, and many more, are embraced within the vast and sweeping panorama of this Swabian spokesman of the Spirit (in this case, of the World Spirit): Georg Wilhelm Friedrich Hegel. It is just that the recognition of how rarely philosophy has risen to the heights of its time, as it has done here, and that in the service of a "thinking consideration" of reality and its elevation to the level of the concept, generally runs along with—paradoxically enough—the no-less-explicit recognition that, in the context of the Hegelian philosophy, this same reality can appear *less intelligible* than it does when we confine ourselves to taking note of what has occurred and merely *keep to the facts*. And it is quite true that we may feel justified in asking rather rhetorically of Hegel, or more precisely, of his writings, what the Barabbas of Pär Lagerkvist once asked with regard to God, namely *why he cannot speak more clearly*. Even a thinker as close in some ways to Hegel as Adorno used to tell his most advanced students (according to a personal reminiscence of Günther Wohlfart) what he expressed to the general reader as follows: "In the realm of great philosophy Hegel is no doubt the only one with whom at times one literally does not know and cannot conclusively determine what is being talked about."[12]

This degree of incomprehensibility, even on the part of thinkers of note, has led certain so-called "neoempiricists" to accuse the Hegelian philosophy—an accusation to me no less incomprehensible—of being nothing but an arbitrary mental construction, a mere *Gedankending* or *ens rationis*, whose highest motto would indeed be "so much the worse for the facts." As if simply keeping to the facts were not, for its part, another fact, just as incomprehensible as the first, given that it would then be necessary to connect both in terms of a *third* fact, and so on ad infinitum. As if the facts explained themselves on their own account and merely bore their rationality within themselves, revealing the latter *gratis et amore* to anyone who was simply content to observe them. As if the facts, in any case, were not in effect a *factum*, something *made*, something whose origin and operation is what reason is called on to account for. As if the facts did not refer us back to a circumstance or situation in the context of which alone these facts can even begin to take on meaning, connection, and coherence. As if the facts, in the end, did not require that we *speak* of them and *think* about them precisely if we wish to respect them and—as it has never better been said—to take *account* of them.

3. A Literal Reading of Hegel

Among these facts, as celebrated and well-known as they are—for that very reason—not genuinely known,[13] one in particular stands out. It is perhaps *the theme* par excellence of the French Revolutionary Terror: the fact that between 1791 and 1794 people would have their heads cut off without more ado, and without any concern at all. If this is so, after the (well-merited) reputation provoked by Hegel's writings in general, it was only to be expected that some would experience relief and others a certain disappointment—in the sense of *tu quoque*—to find the man whom Adorno would describe as *ho skoteinos* or "the obscure one"—as Heraclitus was known in his day—was quite capable of speaking of these things in terms as straightforward and comprehensible as the following: "It is thus the coldest and meanest of all deaths, with no more meaning than that of cutting off a head of cabbage, or of a gulp of water."[14]

My intention, then, in this essay lies precisely in transforming these rather anodyne descriptions into something that is difficult to comprehend—at least for healthy common sense and equally for the abstract understanding (*Verstand*)—for the sake of a better *rational grasp* of the revolutionary *fact* or *act*.

The general assumption that has guided me in this regard is the following: at least in the *Phenomenology of Spirit* and the *Science of Logic* Hegel's writing refuses to observe the established distinctions between the semantic and the nonsemantic, and the categorematic and the noncategorematic. As in the case of the greatest poetry (in that of Friedrich Hölderlin, the friend of Hegel's youth, to say no more), the most productive and appropriate mode of exegesis of Hegel's texts is, in my opinion, to accept that *all* of his expressions (including the specific features of punctuation) are significant (with distinct levels of comprehension that communicate analogically with one another), that they constantly serve to refer back and forth within the most varied of contexts, that they prove, in short, to be as polyvalent as they are incapable of being replaced with or substituted by other terms.[15] If this is the case, then the claim that death (in the period of *la Terreur*) has no more significance than cutting or hacking off (*durchauen*) a head of cabbage (i.e., separating it from the stem that binds it to the earth) or, more precisely, possessing the significance of a gulp of water (*ein Schluck Wassers*) cannot be dismissed without more ado as a mere metaphor, as simply a vivid illustration that draws attention to the indifference with which such a death was commonly registered (or rather its public display in the presence of judges, executioners, and spectators; I imagine that the victims themselves, however accustomed they would also have been to sights and spectacles, certainly did not feel the same indifference). That the Hegelian expressions here should possess, at least *to begin with*, such a normal sense is undeniable. But that they are effectively exhausted in such apparent normality (as if the reading of these words would merely produce the same indifference in the reader as death on the chopping-block or death by water) is surely far more questionable.

Let us observe, first, that just as in other even more famous passages, certain interpreters (Alexandre Kojève, for example) have attempted to smooth down Hegel's own text, assuming that he has committed some grammatical error or other[16]; in this case too there is a temptation to *correct* the text by supposing that something is missing here. Thus even if we are able to accept that the significance of death in the Terror is the same as that of cutting off a head of cabbage (on a proportional analogy based on the feeling that both these actions produce in the one who performs them), it is more difficult to conceive that this death possesses no more significance than that of a gulp of water. For it seems that one would have to add something else. It would surely have to be understood, for example, that such a death would possess no more significance than that of *drinking* a mouthful of water, a verb that Hegel would not specifically have felt it necessary to spell out because the matter in question would be self-evident. Or in other words, the know-it-all who lurks in all of us thinks that the remark *means to say* that death is *like* a gulp of water, not that it *is* a gulp or mouthful of water or is produced by it. Yet on the contrary, what I am maintaining here, and something that is already intended by the very title of this essay, is the need to accept quite literally what Hegel has actually written. And I maintain, moreover, that we have to accept, in effect, that the death proper or peculiar to the Terror, the revolutionary death par excellence, *was and is a gulp of water*. And this is so, not because of how this death may affect the feeling of the spectator (something implicit in a normal reading of the passage), but *in the very sense indicated*, since this gulp or mouthful (and certainly a bad one) is what produces death in the victim of revolutionary Terror.

What is more, it is also worthy of note that, to defend a literal reading of this passage, it struck me as fitting to make this *poetico-holistic* starting point quite explicit, whereas in adopting the other more "standard" interpretive reading no one points out that for this it is necessary to make tacit use of a much more *recherché* and even frivolous assumption that appears to be accepted by everyone without further reflection: the idea that this death by the revolution is or was above all a *spectacle*, one produced and expressly staged "only for the eyes," as we might say (for the eyes, of course, of the French actors and spectators of the time, not for *our* eyes, the eyes of the philosophical consciousness, which, for its part, is confined to "purely looking on" or to a *reines Zusehen*). I believe it was Kant, at least as far as the philosophical profession was concerned, who was largely responsible for this *theatrical* interpretation of events, since for him the French Revolution, as glimpsed from the more-or-less secure and distant "box" of Prussia (especially given that we are talking of East Prussia), was fundamentally precisely that: a *Schauspiel*,[17] even if it aroused approving sentiments in this philosophical spectator, or indeed a moral enthusiasm that was quite different from that indifference denounced by Hegel himself in his early years[18] (with a direct comparison with ancient Rome), and would later be captured in popular form by Dickens in his *Tale of Two Cities*.

This is not how I see the matter, nor do I believe that this was Hegel's principal or *capital* intention (since we are talking of decapitation here) in writing such a seemingly "trite" passage. On the contrary, I suggest that once its vulgar *sense* is grasped (which is certainly possible without that much difficulty), we may proceed to situate its *signification* within the context of the particular phenomenological section on "Absolute Freedom and Terror," and expanding this context, if necessary, for the sake of a greater comprehension of the text to then pass on to a *higher* level of understanding where the initial sense and the further signification are deployed as a *symbolic expression* (taking "symbol" here in the Schellingian rather than the Hegelian sense of the term) for the *logical* conception of the revolutionary fact or "deed."

4. Hegel's Two "Terrors"

Let us first of all consider the issue of "situating" the text at issue (its appropriate *Erörterung*, to use a word dear to Heidegger). Above all, we must insist, once again, on a *literal* reading of the title of the section in question. For it does *not* specifically tell us that revolutionary freedom was or *has been* the Terror (thus understanding the title "Absolute Freedom and Terror" as "absolute freedom *or*, so to speak, the terror"). As I see it, we must take the copulative conjunction "and," in the first place, as indicating a separation (something was and still is the Revolution over and beyond *la Terreur*) and then again as indicating a certain consequence (the Revolution, by virtue of its *philosophical* principles, would effectively result in the Terror). And last of all, though certainly not least, we must recognize that in this text Hegel will allude to *two* Terrors: a direct one that properly arises from the revolutionary events in France, and another indirect and *reflexive* one, so to speak, namely the terror before the death proper to the Terror that would in turn produce, in reaction, a coup d'état that would reconfigure the damaged *materiality* of the "spiritual masses" of before, though now renewed and revitalized under the *form* of the watchwords of liberty, equality, and fraternity as spread abroad under the aegis of Napoleon, and particularly in the period after he became *Consul.*

It is well known, of course, that this section of Hegel's text offers a critical exposition of the *experience* of consciousness in the face of the French Revolution. But if we are to avoid, once again, rather overhasty and somewhat "standard" understandings of this issue, we should point out in advance that the term "experience" (so popular with those who insist that we must stick closely to the *facts*) denotes, in Hegel's eyes, a genetic process. Thus consciousness takes something directly and immediately to be true (what Kant calls "*das Fürwahrhalten*"), and therefore as something that stands before it and is distinct from itself; but when consciousness *assimilates* it in order to be *sure* and *certain* of that which it signifies *for consciousness*, the process generates something alien, something else that is distinct from what was initially presupposed, something that in truth is distinct both with regard to the object and with regard to consciousness itself, thereby producing a split or rupture within consciousness. Now the object is not as it first appeared to consciousness (the initial characteristics of each experience tend to be expressly marked by Hegel by the phrase "it seems" or "it appears," *es scheint*) in a determinate *Gestalt*; now, consciousness is conscious and aware, it takes consciousness or becomes aware—not without a painful sense of frustration—that its expectations have not been fulfilled in the very act of realizing its experience (once again we take literally the expression *in der Tat* with which Hegel also generally concludes each process of experience, an expression usually translated in English as "in fact" but could perhaps best be rendered as "in deed" or "in the event"). With respect to every dialectical "moment" of consciousness, what emerges for the latter is precisely a *katabolē*, a "ruination" in which its expectations are dashed, whereas experience that is fully carried through involves an "integrating and ascending turn," an *anabolē*, along the phenomenological path, or a progressive movement in which Spirit "takes consciousness" or becomes aware of itself in its Other.[19] It is possible, then, to say that the work Hegel published in 1807 effectively expounds, on the one side, a catabolism of consciousness with regard to each of its several shapes, in which consciousness is hopelessly frustrated in the act (*in der Tat*), in the realization of its own experience; and at the same time, on the other side, it also expounds an anabolism, a "molecular" ascent on the part of Spirit (a unitary process, although one that is subjected, through "sublation" or *Aufhebung*, to a form of proportionality that is ever more intense in its antagonistic character. Thus the more the catabolism—the process of disintegration—itself grows, the more powerful becomes the anabolism, the process in which Spirit comes wholly to know itself in its Other, until the point where the reciprocal and *interiorized* acknowledgement of evil—an evil that, if taken as what it is and thus elevated to the level of praxis, would lead to the destruction of society, to civil war—already becomes itself the *reconciliation*. Likewise, analogously, with regard to religion, this is already the death on the Cross, and in turn, the Life of the Spirit in its community. *For us*, the pure contemplation of this "double helix," this chiasmic conjunction, presupposes the process in which this phenomenological metabolism is brought to consciousness.

Here then we find surprising confirmation on Hegel's part, of the well-known revolutionary proclamation (which is before all and above all a *Pauline* one): *the worse* (for consciousness), *the better* (for Spirit). Let us apply this, then, to the relevant passages of our text. The whole text turns, of course, on death, regarded by Hegel as the "absolute Lord"—which had already made an appearance in the famous "struggle for recognition" of chapter IV A: the dialectic of self-consciousness, split between the lordly and the servile consciousness. There Hegel writes: "This consciousness [the servile consciousness—F.D.] has been fearful, not for this or that in particular, not for this instant or that, but its whole being has been seized with dread; for it has experienced the fear of death, the absolute Lord. In that experience it has felt itself inwardly dissolved, has trembled with every fiber of its being, and everything solid and stable has been shaken to its foundations" (*Phä. GW* 9, 114; Miller, 117; translation adapted). Let us note the plastic power of these verbs in the final phrase: in this fear, this terror, consciousness has inwardly *dissolved*, has trembled throughout its being (*durch-aus*), has felt how everything fixed, solid, or stable has been shaken. Yet here, however, this fear before the absolute Lord, in the face of death, springs from the desire of the individual to preserve his *animal* life. In our text from a later point in the *Phenomenology*, by contrast, the terror in the face of death is experienced by a will that is absolutely free, liberated of course from its attachment to animal life; yet free as well from its credo in the broad sense of the word: from its beliefs, traditions, ethnic prejudices; free even, ideally and ultimately, from its social origins: for as Deleuze once put it, reason—enlightened reason—is an erudite conversation between *proprietors*.[20] Thus when the will liberates itself from passion all that is now left, *logically* speaking, is a single passion: the broadest, most original, and most inextinguishable one, the one that is inalienably rooted in every individual—a passion that in being completely the object of the singular self-consciousness (recognized *absolutely* in and by every individual as being one and the same as the *volonté générale* of Rousseau) ends up being that with which the self-conscious will identifies itself, thus becoming, in and through this identification, Subject. This single and radical passion is the *passion of freedom* itself.[21]

Freedom, indeed, but as an absolute entity devoid of any predicate at all (if it were otherwise, if freedom were the power to do this or that thing, it would then be determined *heteronomously*, as Kant would say). Thus, absolute freedom implies an in-determinate, or in-finite, detachment from everything that belongs to the world, whether it derive from the sensible world of political power and economic wealth or from the supersensible world of faith. In Aristotelian terms, it *appears* (*es scheint*) that this freedom were nothing but the positive essence of the personality of every singular self-consciousness (what it must be because this is "what it already was" in its being). Therefore what it has to be will be preserved in that positive essence, *intimior intimo suo*. This is all that self-consciousness can do or know, caught up as it is in the intoxicating experience of absolute freedom and completely divorced from any materiality and any particularity. And this, in effect, is what appears.

Yet *in the event* or "in deed" (*in der Tat*) the process in which such self-consciousness "becomes conscious" of its experience, as Hegel himself says, involves a sudden reversal or *Umschlag*,[22] a catabolic catastrophe in which this "self-thinking" (in a clear allusion to Kant) is suppressed as soon as it realizes itself as pure thinking. Thus while it certainly attempts to "materialize" that *formality*, it does so by applying a form that is indifferent to every particular case, that is, by imposing itself uniformly on and thus uni-formalizing a matter that is thereby taken *eo ipso* as abstract (thus what one does is all the same, for all that counts here is the *good will*, in this identification as it were of Rousseau and Kant). In making itself a "world" (or in terms of the Fichtean *Tathandlung*: when the well-intentioned *Handlung* or "moral action" is converted into a worldly "fact," into a deed [*Tat*]), positivity is turned into *the act* and becomes negativity. What the singular self wanted, through action, was to realize the universal; but what happened is precisely that this universal has literally been *jeopardized*, for the result of the action now appears as something singular in the service of the particular *agent*. It is therefore *logical* that this action finds itself judged negatively by the universal, which suddenly and catastrophically turns into the negation of this particular being of the individual. Now the individual (the will that is absolutely free) had claimed that all of its own particularity should be dissolved, should become the same or equal with everyone else: in short, should become something *abstract*, that is, pure *being* (the abstraction, in effect, of everything determinate). Thus the negative essence is now directed against its own and only being, namely the *being* of the individual (and thereby against its own universal *being*).

This negation of being on the part of the essence, this annihilation of what it is in the name of what it ought to be, is nothing but, and can be nothing but, *death*, the absolute Lord. Thus it is that "fear of the Lord is the beginning of wisdom" (as Hegel loves to repeat from *Proverbs* I, 7: "*timor domini initium sapientiae*").

And this is in truth a literally clarifying and enlightening death since, as Hegel also says in another context, "the fear of the Lord is, indeed, the beginning, but only the beginning, of wisdom."[23] As we have already pointed out, the *katabolē* (*Umschlag*, *katastrophē*) of the experience of absolute freedom is, at the same time, the *anabolē* (*Aufstieg*, *anabasis*) in which it "becomes aware" of the result of this experience. In effect, to offer a highly compressed summary of this inverted *consciousness of experience*, it is clear that the pure self-equality of a freedom without limits (an absolute freedom) is certainly nothing but negation. Yet it is no less clear that to speak of a subsisting form of being (*Bestehen*) that always remains equal or identical to itself is to speak of *substance*. So that exactly what emerges as an absolutely negative result for each singular consciousness *recoils* violently upon this rejuvenated *substance* of self-consciousness in general (in *la Nation une et invisible* that we might describe as the terrestrial expression of the *Être suprême*) and leads it to fragment, to *divide* into spiritual masses, lending to each of them its particular weight and measure (an issue to which I shall return at the end of this essay). This would confer substantial effective reality on freedom, giving weight to it and confirming its limits, in short, converting the *abstract* Nation into a concrete State, and moreover, claiming to turn Europe, in an *imperial* way, into just what Montesquieu had already said that it was, namely *une nation des nations*.

Let us now address, in brief, the phenomenological development of our thematic object. The experience of this shape of consciousness, that of absolute freedom, arises out of the generalized triumph of the principle of *Nüzlichkeit* or utility: the ripest fruit of Enlightenment in that it marks the culmination of a manifest tendency of the Modern Age (we may at least recall the three functions that architecture is supposed to fulfill according to Vitruvius: *utilitas, firmitas, venustas*). In effect, both Descartes[24] in the *Discourse on Method* and Francis Bacon[25] in his *Instauratio magna* insist on the turn from the *vita contemplativa* to the *vita activa*, with a specific view to the transformation of the things of this world: first from "beings" into "objects," and then into useful tools, implements, equipment, and so on (that is, into products or the means of production). And this holds not only for the physical world and the realm of work but also, and perhaps above all, for the political domain, as is clearly revealed both by Rousseau and by Article I of the *Déclaration des droits* of 1789.

This exaltation of utility as the *being of entities* implies of course a process of devaluing the world and depriving it of substance—with regard to both the sensible "physical" world and the supersensible world of faith and scientific insight. And this by virtue of (or by reason of *vertù*, we might more strictly say), by virtue of a general-formal will (a will that is always "right" as Rousseau precisely indicates), a will that is lacking in substance and thus indifferent to whatever it takes up or to whatever particularity that it refuses. It is in this way, to recall a famous observation, that everything solid melts into air: everything, including—at the limit—all our own particular wills. Thus the labor of the negative now turns against these negated "agents of virtue" who inoculate themselves with the *terror of death*. A terror that is entirely necessary, as Hegel shows, precisely as the *terminus medius*, the *Mitte* of the syllogism of Modernity, whose premise as we have seen was utility (the destruction of first nature, whether this be physical or psychical nature), in order to result in the construction of a second nature: *ad extra*, the State (administering a territory subjected to laws); *ad intra*, the inalienable moral conscience (ruling each individual body in the name of the law). We might describe this as an exercise in speculative geopolitics: Hegel is thereby justifying the step from *esprit* to *Geist*, from France to Germany, from Rousseau to Kant: "Just as the realm of the real world passes over into the realm of Faith and Insight, so does absolute freedom leave its self-destroying reality and pass over into another land [*in ein anderes Land*[26]] of self-conscious Spirit where, in this unreal world,[27] freedom has the value of truth" (*Phä. GW* 9, 323; Miller, 363).

This, in its general lines, is the metamorphosis of absolute freedom, the *peripateia* of the Enlightenment (and Kant, as we know, always regarded himself as an *enlightened* thinker): namely, something that *happens* to it. Yet it is not yet an active form of self-limitation (for "to know one's own limit is to know how to sacrifice oneself"[28])—this will only come to pass with the beautiful soul, with the movement of evil and forgiveness.

How then are we to understand this Terror that serves as a *Mitte* between the *new* and the even *newer* age? Let us recall what we said earlier about *narrative symbolism*: the plain significance gives expression to a hidden meaning on another level. And what did the text tell us about death and terror in the face of death? In chapter IV A of the *Phenomenology* we heard how this death *dissolved* the inner and animal substance. In our present context (chapter VI B), by contrast, the corresponding encounter with death is said to be *der kälteste und platteste Tod*, "the coldest and meanest death," which is devoid of all significance. We move here on a level that is nothing but surface, and what transpires on this level is something tasteless and insipid: *like water*. Let us observe, however, that Hegel does not even say that this death is *like* a gulp of water: what he says is that this death has no more significance than cutting off a head of cabbage or taking a gulp of water.

The first of these expressions is an obvious allusion to the guillotine. Then, for a start, we are talking about *a* head. Why is this? Because, where absolute freedom is concerned, nobody is more than anyone: every singular will is already the general will insofar as it abstracts from all of its particularities, from all of its substance. As Rousseau expressly points out in an exercise of arithmetical politics: "but take away from these same wills [i.e. from particular wills] the pluses and minuses that cancel one another, and the general will remains as the sum of the differences."[29] This is an idea that Hegel transposes onto the conceptual level: "Before the universal can perform a deed it must concentrate itself into the One of individuality." Or what amounts to the same thing: the general will can only be realized in the world of the particular by means of the singular will, and thus "put at the head [*an die Spitze*] an individual self-consciousness; for the universal will is only an *actual* will in a self, which is a One" (ibid.).

But in that case the other singular ones find themselves excluded from the whole and they, taken together, see it as a crime—*ein*

Verbrechen, a violation of the universal—that one individual, one head as it were, should assume the position of the government; for the one who governs, on the other hand, all the other individuals, that is, all the other heads, become objects of suspicion: "When the universal will maintains that what the government has actually done is a crime committed against it, the government, for its part, has nothing specific or outwardly apparent by which the guilt of the will opposed to it could be demonstrated; for what stands opposed to it as the *actual* universal will is only an unreal pure will, *intention*. *Being suspected*, therefore, takes the place, or has the significance and effect, of *being guilty*; and the external reaction against this reality that lies in the simple inwardness of intention, consists in the cold, matter-of-fact annihilation of this existent self, from which nothing else can be taken away but its mere being" (*Phä*. *GW* 9, 320; Miller, 360). Hence the ensuing struggle between different factions, the unexpected product of the impossible task of trying to ensure that the sovereignty of the people should reside in each and every one of the citizens. As Saint Just proclaimed: "The sovereignty of the people demands that this latter be united; hence it is opposed to all factions: every faction is, for this reason, an attack on sovereignty [. . . .] Today factions are a crime since they isolate liberty and diminish the influence of the people." Thus democracy taken to an extreme ends up in tyranny, whether this is exercised by an individual human being or a small group of special individuals who turn themselves into *the voice of the people*. Therefore, as Saint Just concludes, "to elude the snares of our enemies you shall unite as one sovereign [*en état de souverain*] in order to resist all parties."[30] The subject of this apostrophe is the French People, yet the one who exhorts them in this way is a particular citizen who claims to have renounced his particularity in order to identify with and submerge himself in this "united people." He urges that the People become what it already *essentially* is. But if he demands this of the people just as he is, namely as *citizen* Saint Just, then he is usurping the sovereignty of the nation. And if he demands it qua voice of the people, then neither the harangue itself nor the rejection of all parties (of all *other* parties) makes no sense, for the Sovereign People is already united and doesn't need anyone to tell it what it must do or how it must be constituted. And here we confront a dilemma that persists to this day in every authoritarian democracy that wavers between the principle of "All for One" and "One for All"[31]: either the sacrifice of all, who delegate authority to One as long as he is like them: to *anyone*, or the absorption of the individual in the social body—either dictatorship or the masses. In both cases, the individual as singular self (or as result of the dialectical interaction of the universal and the particular) disappears. Even the distinction that marks the tyrant turns out to be illusory, since he himself has being only through the *abstract* negation of all the others.

Hegel was admirably quick to appreciate the sudden and catastrophic inversion of absolute freedom into *pure terror*: "But in this way *all other individuals* are excluded from the entirety (*Ganzen*) of this deed and have only a limited share in it, so that the deed would not be a deed of the actual universal self-consciousness. Universal freedom, therefore, can produce neither a positive work nor a deed; there is left for it only *negative* action; it is merely the *fury* of destruction or disappearance" (*Phä. GW* 9, 319; Miller, 359). Not even the man who works the guillotine can obtain a sort of "negative satisfaction" for having cut off the head of the king or the queen, for example, since after the Revolution both such figures have lost any meaning. In this particular case, the exhortations of Nietzsche's "Madman" (*der tolle Mensch*), calling on human beings to assume their responsibility for having murdered God, would have no meaning whatsoever.[32] All this would have no meaning because Louis XVI, demoted *malgré lui* to a mere *citoyen*, and one moreover who has betrayed the Revolution by attempted flight, has ceased to be the dynastic vessel of divine power, and because God himself has been transformed, in the revolutionary period, into a bloodless and immortal nonentity, into *l'Être suprême*.

Thus, all heads are equal, indifferent to one another, empty in their own right (*für sich*): a matter of pure punctuality, of indeterminate continuity (like the balloon-heads in the paintings of Giorgio de Chirico)—and that by the action of the guillotine, a point—a dot—separated from an "i" that collapses. But why precisely by means of the guillotine? Surely on account of its characteristic speed, economy, efficiency, cleanliness, and—above all—its mercy, given that the act of execution itself is painless and can be completed in less than a minute. In fact, it seems that the mechanical action of the guillotine is so quick that the head remains conscious for a number of seconds after being severed. What is more, Dr. Antoine Louis, of the Academy of Surgery, changed the horizontal blade for a slanting one which was more effective for cutting (at the request of Louis XVI, indeed, so that the executioners would not suffer any harm). But the fundamental thing is this: "The Constitutional Assembly adopted the use of the guillotine *so that the death penalty should be the same for all, regardless of rank or social class.*"[33] In short, just like *cutting off heads of cabbage.*

5. Metal and Water: Beheading and Drowning

If, then, this cold and clean cut turns the human head into a bit of vegetable, can there possibly be any hidden meaning, within the Hegelian system, which connects these *metallic* characteristics of the blade with the mass character of death in the Revolution? I believe there is, though to elucidate this point we shall have to turn to a rather unexpected source, namely to Hegel's *philosophy of nature.* And it is almost as if we wished to establish a rigorous counterpart to the *plural* indifference of those severed heads (logically speaking: the multiple "ones," *abstractly negated*—or *"repelled"*—by the *One*[34]). For there Hegel specifically says that metal is an individuality that is abstractly indifferent and equal-to-itself, something that is substantially uniform: an impenetrable being-for-self, singular and punctiform in character (*Enz.* §304, *Anm.*; Petry, vol. II, 84f.). In this regard, these observations from Hegel's philosophy of nature are capable, *in retrospect,* of shedding considerable light on the "death" by execution that we find in the revolutionary context: abstractly indifferent substantiality in the face of the neutral and insubstantial character of the executed. Thus Hegel writes: "Metals, on the other hand, as they are not neutral bodies but are abstractly indifferent, tend to be confined to formal configuration (*formelle Gestalt*) [. . . .] Metal still remains substantially uniform" (*Enz.* §315, *Zusatz*; Petry, II, 116; translation adapted). And if anyone were to doubt the intimate connection of the metallic with being-for-self, with the logical One, and of the latter with the revolutionary instrument of death, Hegel points out that metal, in contrast to crystals, is "opaque [*undurchsichtig*] because here the individual self [*das individuelle Selbst*], by virtue of its higher specific gravity,[35] is concentrated upon becoming for-itself." We should note the evident metonymy here: the one who is condemned proves to be as indifferent in its punctual character as the guillotine itself (the negative essence). And then again, the multiple and equivalent heads, all of them "equalized" by cutting (*ausgeglichen* or "brought to the same level"—we should not miss the ambivalent irony of the German verb here: *ausgleichen*—correspond to the Head of the "One of individuality" (*das Eins der Individualität*), which, in every case, stands at the head. He, the Governing One—the indifferent and transferable incarnation of the People—is really individual, punctualized, because he *bestows death*. It is a negative life, a pure point: the juncture where that which is elementary or generic and the course of a particular life are divided—cut apart—through the intentional action of the singular One.[36]

Up until this point, the significance of death is taken to be the same as cutting off a head of cabbage. But in the preceding note we have already observed that the "other" death—the *gulp of water*—is bound up with the spectacular *return* of the individual to the realm of the elemental and generic. In this sense, the death *produced* by the gulp of water (not simply the response to death on the part of the executioner: *as if* the one who carries it out were just taking a drink of water) possesses a philosophical meaning higher than that of the *metallic* death that is exercised on a vegetable. And it has this meaning precisely because the *physical* return to the highest example of dissolution, that which is due to the *liquid element* (cold, flat, horizontal) corresponds exactly on its own level to the *spiritual* dissolution of every particular will at the heart of *absolute freedom*. And just as the dissolution in water can lead to a chemical *transformation*, so too, as we shall see, the dissolution of freedom in the revolution through *hydrological* death could lead—and did in fact lead—in political terms to the changes during the *Thermidore* (1794) and in moral terms to the conceptual internalization of *Fichtean* ethics (also in 1794).

But why, precisely, speak of water here? On Christmas Eve 1794, Hegel, always well informed about unfolding events in France, wrote a letter to Schelling that was also meant for his other friends from the Tübingen Stift: "You probably know that Carrier has been guillotined. Do you still read the French press? [. . .] This trial is very important, and has revealed the complete ignominy of Robespierre's party."[37] The "business" to which Hegel alludes here marked the beginning of the end of the period of the Terror, when along with Carrier and other Jacobins, Saint Just and Robespierre himself were executed. Now among the terrible excesses of the time, the name of Jean-Baptiste Carrier stands out with a certain sinister brilliance. It is not particularly strange, therefore, that Hegel should mention him. But it is even less strange, as I shall try to show, that he may also serve as an excellent example and guide to explain the metamorphosis of absolute freedom in the Terror *by means of water.*

Carrier, a member of the *Convention Nationale*, arrived in Nantes in September 1793. He soon made a name for himself as the successful inventor of "*déportation verticale*," the process whereby the revolutionary terror was applied to the provinces. The particular procedure he devised was much more economic, efficient, and, above all, quicker than the guillotine which, after all, can only dispatch one person at a time. What is more, the prisons in Nantes were packed and cases of typhus had already been identified there. Why, then, cannot we generalize the singular rather than singularizing the generic, with the added risk of converting the exemplary spectacle into the danger—between pity and fear—of inciting the revulsion of the people, of the "many ones" who have not yet been executed, against the One (generically connected to that which is One: absolute and negative freedom)? Why not just dissolve the individuals, without even having to collect the corpses and clean up the scaffold afterward? And in effect it was Carrier who introduced *les noyades*: the mass drownings in the Loire, which was deep and narrow as it snaked through Nantes with its powerful eddies. For this purpose, he employed barges fitted with trapdoors which are opened once the vessel is right in the middle of the current. The victims (literally displaced or banished from the land: consigned to water), hands tied behind their backs, plunge into the depths. And that is that. Little barks of salvation in reverse, as we might say today, serving as they did to transfer people from land to water. In four months alone Carrier carried out seven of these *noyades*, and it is estimated that he exterminated some 2,000 human beings in this way[38]: an early model of efficiency, comparable only with the Nazi death ovens, and a method that would later be technologically refined—with airplanes instead of barges—when Argentinean detainees were thrown out over the Rio de la Plata during the military rule of the Colonels.

But Carrier committed an unpardonable error, from the political (and also *logical*) point of view by perverting the course of justice, profiting from his connections with the general order (la Convention) to *particularize* his own *singularity* and claiming control of the wealth of many of the Nantes nobility by the simple means of accusing them of having betrayed the Revolution. When the nobles, after being transported to Paris, were nonetheless absolved of the charge, Carrier turned against Robespierre himself but was consequently condemned by his own faction and summarily executed—this time by guillotine: a sign of distinction in the end. His head rolled on 6 February 1794, and Robespierre would be executed on 27 July of the same year. La Convention drowns its enemies and decapitates its sons.

But why, in philosophical terms, should water be more "advantageous" than steel for bringing the step that leads from freedom to terror to the level of the concept? Let us examine how this can be. The body of the drowned individual assumes an indifferent equality, a self-sameness (the essential relation of inner and outer): the element of water—the generic and dissolvent element—is separated from itself only when the surface is temporarily broken and penetrated, as the body returns to a pure condition of envelopment that separates the same from the same, what is equal from what is equal. In contrast to the presence of the decapitated body, which arouses pity, incites horror, or cries out for vengeance, even in the most absurd way (like Lucille before the corpse of Desmoulins, as Büchner and Celan have unforgettably recalled for us), the bodies of the drowned disappear from sight—to be devoured by fish or to float way into the sea.

To be sure, these hydrological atrocities are not—or are not only—a product of a perverse or depraved mentality, for they are one of the dialectical products of the "liquefaction" of the world in accordance with a certain ideal of the Enlightenment, with the consequent vanishing of the *solidity*, *opacity*, and *stability* of a world that has now evaporated.[39] For the *Lebensstellung*, the place in life, that Marx will celebrate so unreflectively fifty years later, would have to be regarded, from the Hegelian point of view, as a pure oscillation between the individual will and the general will that can only be resolved through a *negative infinite judgment*. This is a living attitude that, in death, and after death, also returns in a negative way, as *revenant* or specter.

In this regard one could say that the Marxian position represents a regress and a reversion, not only—as I have indicated—to the attitude of Kant (passing, however, from being a "spectator" to wishing to be the promoter and fulfiller of a revolution that was regarded merely as a beginning), but also to the attitude of the early Hegel himself. Rosenkranz recounts something of this unparalleled alliance between revolutionary enthusiasm and Kantian idealism that was so strongly felt at the Stift at the beginning of the 1790s. There was an obvious Kantian inspiration behind the idea that only a prior revolution in our entire "mode of thought" (*Denkungsart*) could lead to any successful revolution in the world outside, one that would thus avoid or at least alleviate the struggle between different factions and the terroristic dangers of a political state on the brink of collapse or decomposition: "The bloody spectre of the Terror did not prevent enthusiasm for the spectacle of seeing a State coming into being on the basis of the idea of the State, on the basis of the powers essential for its existence" (Ros., 32).

6. Fanaticism as a Chemical Precipitate

Considered in this light, the French Revolution would appear as the real incarnation of an *onto-politological* argument, as we might put it, one that marks the passage from essence to existence on the part of the concept. In 1806 the *incipit*, though no more than that, of this great event is still celebrated as "the truth of Enlightenment." For, in effect, the two worlds, the world of truth and the world of the actuality and the present, have united as one in the relation between being-for-another and being-for-self (the self-consciousness that finds its true knowledge in being-for-another): "The two worlds are reconciled and heaven has been transplanted to the earth below."[40] Nonetheless, the young Hegel was already clearly aware that victims would be needed if this fruitful transplantation were to be achieved. In this regard it is difficult to read a letter from Hegel to Schelling of 1795 without seeing it precisely as an anticipation *in nuce* of his subsequent phenomenological critique of the Terror and its metamorphosis in post-Kantian *Moralität*. Hegel writes to his friend Schelling that "the enlivening power of ideas [. . .] will lift hearts, which will learn to make sacrifices for such ideas [*ihnen aufzuopfern*]. For the spirit of constitutions has precisely made a pact with self-interest and founded its realm upon it."[41]

In any case, it seems as though this confidence in the achievements of the revolution and the acceptance of the necessity of victims for the sake of its realization did not survive the *Wanderjahre* of the young Hegel, the years of his forced "pilgrimage" as a personal tutor. And we cannot rule out the possibility that the period when he lived in such close proximity to Hölderlin in Frankfurt, at the very moment when the poet was completing the final version of his novel *Hyperion*, exercised a significant influence on his changing attitude in this regard. We may recall Hölderlin's words: "Whenever human beings have attempted to turn the State into Heaven, they have only transformed it into Hell."[42] Hegel's so-called *Wastebook*, which includes the various aphorisms that he composed during the Jena period, also provides evidence of this change of outlook. It is quite true, as we have already seen in connection with Carrier, that the philosopher's view regarding the "followers of Robespierre" was never particularly favorable. But now we could say that this perspective has been "raised to the concept," and clearly prefigures the phenomenological analysis that is to come (along with an allusion to the covert connection between the *being* of Robespierre and the *I* of Fichte): "Robespierre's answer to everything—if someone here had thought this or done that, desired this or said that—was: *la mort!*

This soon becomes tedious in its uniformity, yet it works for everything. [. . .] I can kill everything, or abstract from everything. Thus this stubborness [*Eigensinn*] cannot be overcome, and can overcome everything within itself.[43] Yet the highest thing that would have to be overcome is just this freedom, this death itself" (Ros., 542f).

On the other hand, this feeling of revulsion in the face of *la fièvre terroriste* had even come to be shared by the members of the Convention Nationale itself. It is true that the highest place of (dis)honor as far as the revolutionary *machine à tuer* is concerned must undoubtedly go to *les noyades* of Nantes, though the reek of spilled blood infected many other places too: in Toulouse, in Albi, in Cahors, and throughout the region of the Loire. It is said that Danton, raving and perhaps already suspecting that he himself was about to fall, had declared to Camille Desmoulins (leader of the Club des Cordeliers, yet another illustrious victim): "Ah! c'est trop de sang versé! Regarde: la Seine coule de sang!" What is more, it appears that even Robespierre had murmured among his closest collaborators in disgust: "Quoi, toujours de sang!"[44]

In this regard, it is highly characteristic of the mature Hegel to emphasize the *Umschlag*, the sudden turn or reversal of things. The philosopher admits, of course, the necessity of the triumph of the "abstract understanding," this "tremendous power of the negative,"[45] and celebrates it; yet in this very triumph he also sees how this freedom "turns" into death; or, expressed in chemical terms, the precipitation of fire as water. Thus his praise for the *philosophes* of the Enlightenment can sometimes border on the dithyrambic: "These men heroically defended, with genius, with warmth, with fire, with spirit, and with valor, the mighty human right to subjective freedom, to their views and convictions: for these men it is one's own I, the human spirit, that is the source [*Quelle*] of all that man must acknowledge and respect."[46] Yet at this point (and indeed never more effectively) Hegel completely inverts the praise into critique. For such a "ardent" defence of (solely) *subjective* freedom immediately implies a certain fanaticism: "Hence the fanaticism of abstract thought which reveals itself in these thinkers."

And we may say the same for Hegel's extremely famous comparison of the Revolution with daybreak, which is repeated in his lectures on *Weltgeschichte*, at least from 1822 onward: "This was therefore a glorious spiritual dawn. All thinking beings shared in the jubilation of this epoch. Sublime emotions stirred men's minds at this time; a spiritual enthusiasm shook the world, as if the actual reconciliation of the divine with the world was now accomplished for the first time."[47] In the preceding footnote I have already drawn attention to the *caveat*, the care with which Hegel here observes the practice of *relata refero*. So it was believed in that epoch, something that was, in effect, a *Sonnenaufgang*. But the revolution was only that: the dawn, the sunrise, but certainly not the *zenith*. Hegel expresses himself with greater clarity in the *Encyclopaedia* (and here we are talking about the *ipsa verba magistri*, rather than just the words of his lectures as recorded by the students who attended them). Once again he praises the event as a "dawn, a sunrise." And, precisely as such an *incipit*, he speaks of "the *youthful* pleasure in the new epoch that has blossomed both in the realm of science and in the political realm [. . .] this pleasure greeted the dawn (*Morgenröte*) of the rejuvenated spirit with *intoxication*."[48]

How then was it possible to pass from the fire and the wine, intoxicating as they are, to the sober activities of drinking and gulping water with a certain taste of blood? It was possible because, from the political, or better, from the phenomenological point of view, absolute freedom makes mass execution unavoidable, since, faced with the abstract universal (the Supreme Being, the Nation, the I, and ultimately Death), every individual, precisely by being an individual (through being *rooted* in nature, particularized, and distinctive), is guilty. Yet the reason for this too is, in accordance with Hegel's speculations in the *Philosophy of Nature*, that *water is nothing but fire that has been extinguished*. Up until to this point it is clear that the political and the chemical perspective are *logically* connected in Hegel: in the last analysis, the revolution cannot exist without the political correlate of the *galvanic pile* in the electrochemical context, namely a metallic process of oxidization and reduction. It was not for nothing that Volta described the pile that he developed and perfected as a "source of perpetual power."[49]

And in effect, if the interpretations provided by Hegel in his *Philosophy of Nature* (in his attempt to raise the phenomenon to the level of the concept) are difficult to accept in a scientific context, they nonetheless prove particularly helpful for comprehending the hidden presuppositions involved in his evaluation and critique of the Revolution and the Terror. With regard to the point that principally interests us here: the metaphorical exploitation of the transition from fire (the ardent commitment of the *philosophes* and the earliest revolutionaries) to water (the flat indifference of deaths en masse). It is obvious, of course, that the scientific analyses of fire cast a vivid light (as we would only expect) on the Enlightenment (*l'Âge des Lumières!*), or on the triumph of pure Insight (*Einsicht*) regarding the sensible world and the world of faith. One only has to consider the following passage from the *Encyclopaedia*: "That which is consumed by fire is, firstly, the concrete [*mutatis mutandis*, the sensible world—F.D.], and then that which stands opposed to it [the supersensible world—F.D.]. To consume concrete being is to bring it into opposition, to animate or ignite it [*es begeisten, es befeuern*—literally to spiritualize it, to inflame it]. [. . .] In this way concrete being is brought to the extreme point of consuming itself, and thus into a state of tension with what is other."[50] Up until this point it is the process of oxidization (*mutatis mutandis*, of inflamed revolutionary sentiment—F.D.). Here, in accordance with the *Umschlag* we have already emphasized, the process that has reached its extreme point suddenly, in a paroxysm, turns into its opposite: into *reduction*, that is, into the production of *water*. "The other aspect [namely the reduction—F.D.] of this process is that the determinate, differentiated, and individualized particularity [here let us remember the 'distinction,' in terms of blood and wealth alike, that belongs to the Nantes nobility—F.D.], which is present in all concrete being is reduced to the unity and indeterminateness of neutrality. This why every chemical process will produce water and give rise to opposition [*So soll jeder Prozess der Chemie Wasser produzieren, so wie er Entgegensetzung hervorbringt*] [. . . .] The neutrality into which fire subsides, and by which it extinguished is water" (ibid.).

And it is precisely the absolute lack of cohesion, the *fluid* character of water that makes the latter irresistible, for all "punctual" pressure is external to it, and thus communicates itself instantly to all points of the fluid (elasticity), thereby resulting in pure horizontality (cf. *Enz.* §284; Petry II, 39f.). Water thus signifies, in chemical terms, the same as "the emptiness of that syllable" (*Plattheit dieser Silbe*): namely "death." (*Phä. GW* 9, 320; Miller, 360).

We have been comparing the way the unfolding of "absolute freedom and terror" in the *Phenomenology* with passages from the *Philosophy of Nature* that are concerned with metals, with water and fire. If this comparison proves in any way convincing, then it seems we must conclude that the terror, rather than being some kind of perversion of the revolution, is actually a necessary consequence of it: the *Umschlag* of the abstractly conceived good into an absolute evil, and this, of course, despite the *best, the purest, and the most noble intentions* that were harbored by the revolutionaries themselves, and by any revolutionary whatsoever: then, and now.

7. An Inverted Allegory of the Cave

To begin with, as an illustration of this, we cannot do better than cite an account from Hegel's own hand, as recorded by his biographer Rosenkranz, a text from the Jena period that is naturally much concerned with water, and provides a kind of inversion of the famous Platonic simile of the cave. Hegel describes a subterranean community who are not of course in chains; on the contrary, all of its members are united in the same spirit, and they all work for themselves, though at the same time they equally work for the common good: all of them form a single Self, and share a single will. In a constant struggle with nature they strive to hollow out and thus extend their cave continually to create more space where they may peacefully coexist.[51] It is just that with this disappearance of the rock (we remember: all that is solid vanishes into air), with this continual expansion of the cavity, in the end all that is left is *pure vacancy*. The first symptom that something is going badly is a change in the elasticity of the air, for now, of course, it is more rarified. The unease (*Unbehagen*) among the subterranean dwellers thus begins to mount; but instead of stopping to reflect, they struggle to work even more quickly, that is, to demolish everything that still remains dense and opaque (compare the *Umschlag* of the

Revolution within France into a continual *war of conquest* against the powers of the *Ancien Régime*), "with the intent of improving their subterranean condition." Until suddenly "the skin of the earth becomes transparent" (*die Rinde wird durchsichtig*). It turns out that the cave was situated right under a lake. The one at the front cries out in desperation: "Water!" But it is too late: "The lake rushes in and drinks them up [*ertränkt*] even as it gives them drink [*tränkt*]."[52]

Is this anything but a macabre joke, or worse, a reactionary critique of any attempt to establish a just society in the struggle with nature? Yet Hegel is rightly known for his constant hostility to nature and even a certain disdain for nature.[53] I actually believe that Hegel's critique here is essentially directed against the *vacuity* (there is no better word) of revolutionary efforts that consist in mere *destruction*; in fact we cannot even say that these subterranean ones *work*, that is to say, confer form on matter to *inspirit* and *inflame* it (as this will be celebrated by contrast at the end of the path of spirit, in the reconciliation of acting conscience and the beautiful soul). The opacity of stone and the transparent inconstancy of water are two sides of the same coin, the same *abstraction*: that of a gross materialism (hard and opaque like stone) and that of an idealism that clings to the understanding (dissolvent like water). So, to continue with the story, these higher waters have been canalized, collected, and released according to the measure and proportion of the cave below, have provided water to drink and water for the fields; on the other hand, when the earth, by means of fire (the ardent activity of the subterranean people), turns into air (in the ever-more-hollow and extended cave), it opens the way for the water and converts the transparent cavity into a heap of debris and bodies all chaotically submerged with one another. Thus Hegel's little story could serve very well as a prephilosophical illustration of what transpired in France between the Revolution (July 1789) and the reaction of the political center during the Thermidor (the end of July 1794).

Did revolutionary France resolve the problem of the Terror? Curiously enough, in the *Phenomenology* Hegel does not seem to have presented any subsequent shape of consciousness to capture Napoleon and his coup d'état of the 18 Brumaire (1790), although his literally *attractive* personality worked in the opposite direction with regard to the One and the "many ones," ensuring that the people could coagulate around *la tête et l'epée*, to use the felicitous epithet that Sieyès applied to him. Nonetheless, if we pay closer attention to the result of Napoleon's political interventions (admirably exemplified by the *Code civile*) than to his military successes, we might well think that the following text does allude to the task of reunification *ad intra* that Napoleon undertook to accomplish: "in so far as this Substance [in other words: *la Nation*, as conceived by the abstract understanding—F.D.] has shown itself to be the negative element for the individual consciousness, the organization of spiritual 'masses' or spheres [the particular 'estates'—F.D.] to which the plurality of individual consciousnesses are assigned thus takes shape once more. These individuals who have felt the fear of death, of their absolute master, again submit to negation and distinctions, arrange themselves in the various spheres, and return to an apportioned and limited task, but thereby to their substantial unity (namely: the modern State)" (*Phä. GW* 9, 321; Miller, 361).

In any case, as we can infer from this text, in 1806 it seems that Hegel is more concerned to emphasize the conscious and shared action of the individual consciousnesses (i.e., of the *citoyens*) than their subjection to the emperor, as if this return to order and stability had been produced spontaneously. One might have greater reason to understand the text in this way if it had been composed ten years earlier, as if Hegel were here responding more to the philosophic-political conceptions that Kant expressed in his essay *Towards Perpetual Peace* (1795) than to the historical events that Hegel himself experienced *hautnah* in Jena. In effect, Kant had indicated that it is terror in the face of anarchy that brings the people to unite around a *republic*, their *rational mother* (thus abandoning nature: the *stepmother* who has guided them up until now); the republic in which the principal exhortation is: "There shall be no war among us."[54] It is evident that if we accept Rousseau's general definition of a "republic" in this case,[55] Kant's text could have been endorsed by Hegel, given the obvious analogy between the content of that piece and this political reorganization with its "return to an apportioned and limited task."

And it is the case, as we already indicated in relation to the work of the Enlightenment and the corresponding experience of consciousness, that the phenomenological evaluation of absolute freedom and the terror is also twofold: on the one hand, in effect, the French Revolution would have been absolutely necessary, given that the labor of eliminating the substance of external reality leads to the establishment and recognition (through a process of violence, it is true) of *another* substance: the ethical substance of the State, which in the beginning is certainly only regarded subjectively from the side of self-consciousness, a self-consciousness that beholds its own work in this *Furie des Verschwindens* that eliminates its previous world (a natural one, given that aristocratic and dynastic prerogatives are based on blood and lineage). The world now ceases to be alien to self-consciousness precisely because it is the result of its free and conscious action: it is now its world, the world produced by the human will—"the system of right is the realm of freedom made actual, the world of spirit brought forth out of itself as a second nature."[56] When all is said and done, Aristotle had already declared that "the free man is one who is for the sake of himself rather than for the sake of another" (*anthropos* [. . .] *eleutheros ho autou heneka kai mē allou on*).[57] And as with the Stagyrite, so too with Hegel, the free man is one who exists "for himself" (*für sich*) rather than "for another." And similarly for Hegel: (1) political freedom (protected by Right) is based on the metaphysical freedom of being for itself, and (2) the political structures are determined in their content by the "end": namely that of making the realization of human being and human freedom possible.

Be that as it may, it is quite certain, if we are to follow Hegel (and not only in the *Phenomenology*), that the French Revolution developed a specific awareness of the problem involved (to find juridical form for the kind of freedom and order that will make it possible for the individual to become "for himself" and realize a human destiny in the context of the community). But rather than succeeding in effectively resolving this problem, it could not *fail* to bring about tyranny and terror.

Nonetheless, it would be unjust to describe Hegel (after 1814, of course) as the "Philosopher of the Restoration." Quite the contrary:

the Restoration, according to him, was only the abstract negation of the Revolution. In the *Ständeschrift* of 1817, as we know, Hegel passed harsh judgment on the *Remigranten*, the reactionaries who returned to France after the defeat of Napoleon, filled as they were with hatred and the desire for revenge. These people, Hegel tells us, "have forgotten nothing and learnt nothing," but "seem to have slept through the last twenty-five years" (namely since the proclamation of the Republic in 1792), which are "possibly the richest which universal history has had, and for us the most instructive, because it is to them that our world and our ideas belong."[58]

And earlier in the same essay, which was directed against the Estates of Württemberg that had chosen to reject the constitution that the king was proposing and were insisting instead on their traditional rights and privileges, Hegel claims that the Estates offer "at one extreme the rigid adherence to the positive constitutional law of a bygone situation" (the same kind of accusation that Hegel leveled at the Holy Roman Empire of the German Nation in 1801). It thus represents the very "opposite of what started twenty-five years ago in a neighboring realm and what at the time re-echoed in all heads, namely that in a political constitution nothing should be recognized as valid unless its recognition accorded with the right of reason [*nichts als gültig anerkannt werden sole, als was nach dem Recht der Vernunft anzuerkennen sey*]."[59]

8. From Absolute Negativity to the Element of Freedom

It has already been emphasized that what was in question here was only a *beginning* rather than a fulfilment. An undertaking that was framed solely in terms of the abstract understanding can only be realized in accordance with the same *dissolvent* abstraction. And we also know, phenomenologically speaking, that it was the (subjective) terror in the face of the (regime of) terror (in other words: a concrete feeling, a reaction in the face of an abstraction of the understanding) that meant, *at the level of thought*, that subjectivity would have to pass over "into another land [*in ein anderes Land*]." But is there also a *logical* explanation of the step from the regime of terror to a political constitution governed by the "right of reason." Indeed there is. And Hegel provided it seven years later in the *Science of Logic*, and specifically in the second part, the Doctrine of Essence, which he composed during his time in Nuremberg, when he speaks of the transition from absolute necessity (the blind fate described by Hegel as *Lichtscheu* or "light-shy") to the element of freedom (*das Freie*), there where the negativity of the Self, the death that dissolves all meaning within itself, is converted into the absolutely positive.

In this crucial text (for which I shall provide a very brief commentary inserted in parenthesis as we proceed) we are presented on the one hand with "necessity" as the "*form of the absolute*, the unity of being and essence, simple immediacy which is absolute negativity." On the other hand, "its differences [that which this negativity *differentiates, repels from itself*—F.D.]," are "*an existing manifoldness*" [the individuals, groups, and regions—F.D.] as "a differentiated actuality in the shape of other things independently subsisting over against one another." Each of these things, closed within itself, is involved solely with its own being, so that any contact between them thus "appears as an empty externality." Since their being is that of absolute identity, none involves or concerns the possible particularities of the others, coinciding with them only in being equally self-enclosed, held within an essence that is as necessary as it is abstract (the Nation, a reflection in turn of the Supreme being or of the *supreme essence*— F. D). Each one is free, as long as it does not act in any way (that would involve contaminating the universality of its own inner and self-identical essence—F.D.). As Hegel vividly puts it, this absolute negativity "is the *freedom* of their reflectionless immediacy [*scheinlos*: matt or devoid of 'show']." However, precisely through coinciding in their *general* form (each free individual is and feels itself to be an *enfant de la patrie*—F.D.), these individualities present a determinate content, a distinction that threatens that form: the "mark" that necessity "impressed upon them by letting them go free as absolutely actual [*entliess*: released them]," this same mark that absolute necessity now appeals to (exhorting the citizens to die for their country, whether heroically, on the front line, or as a traitor on the scaffold—F.D.), "as witness to its right and, overcome by it, the actualities now perish." Until this point, the logical transcription of *la Terreur*: "the manifestation of what *determinateness* [for example, the distinctions of the Estates—F. D] is in its truth, that it is negative self-reference, is a *blind* collapse into otherness; [yet] in the sphere of immediate existence [the citizens—F.D.] it is [. . .] a *becoming*, or a *transition* of being into nothing [of life into death—F.D.]" (ibid.). Let us here recall the *Umschlag*: "But, conversely, *being* is equally *essence* [that is: the Nation only *exists* in each one of the citizens, not as a cold abstraction of the understanding, of the law—F.D.], and *becoming* is *reflection* or a *shining* [exhibiting its particular features—F.D.]. Thus the externality is its inwardness [i.e., the national essence appears only as the thought and work of the citizens—F.D.], [. . .] and the *transition* of the actual into the possible, of being into nothing, is a *self-rejoining* [of the existence of each individual within the common essence, and vice versa—F.D.]; [. . .] This identity *of being with itself* in its negation is now *substance*" (*WdL*, *GW* 11, 391–92; Di Giovanni, 487–88). Expressed in political terms, this is the modern State. We should observe that there is no question of any "restoration" here. Nothing has remained as it was before. It is only through attachment and compliance to the *Constitution* (to the *Verfassung*, the mode of thinking and living that remains close to the people, in contrast to a mere *Konstitution* or *Charter*), or in other words, it is only by negating *in particular* (rather than abstractly, rather than through death) one's own particular being (namely the historical and traditional regions of France now reorganized in conformity with the *intellectual* language of the *Départments*) that the *bourgeois* leaves behind the form of an essentially dynastic regime and finds (finds itself in) a true *res publica*. The parallel with the corresponding passage in the *Phenomenology* (the last paragraph of the section "Absolute Freedom and Terror") is evident: "Absolute freedom has thus removed the opposition between the general will and the individual will. The self-alienated Spirit, driven to the extreme of its opposition in which pure willing and the pure agent of that willing [*das reine Wollen und das rein Wollende*] are still distinct, reduces the opposition to a transparent form and therein finds itself" (*Phä. GW* 9, 323; Miller, 363). In effect, therefore, it is *natural* to think that the synthesis of the cold understanding (in chemical terms: water) and ardent sentiment (fire) will lead at last to the substantial rationality of the modern State: the synthesis of the family, of *Heimat*, and civil society, as this will be presented in the *Encyclopaedia* and the *Philosophy of Right*.

Nonetheless, phenomenologically speaking, the experience of the Terror can lead, indeed, to the modern *bourgeois* State, but not to the conscious establishment of a *community* (a *Gemeinschaft*, not yet, however, a *Gemeinde*) based on the interaction of self-consciousnesses that are reconciled, chiasmatically, with the "real" world and with the spiritual "essence." And it cannot do so, for this experience is expressed in the "turn" from an infinite negative judgment (the crime against the nation that reveals that the individual is no more than that: individual—*the singular is singular*—instead of one who participates in the common cause, in the national essence) into an infinite positive judgment (the Nation is only the Nation—*the universal is universal* (cf. *WdL. GW* 12, 70; Di Giovanni, 567). And reflection on this Umschlag can lead, in effect, to the judgment of reflection, and even to its highest formulation as the universal judgment (cf. *WdL. GW* 12, 75ff.; Di Giovanni, 572ff.). Thus, we might say: "All and every one of the citizens constitute the French Nation," which is in fact what is declared by the Constitution of 24 June 1793, which opens with the definition: "The French Republic is one and indivisible." It then proceeds to decide who is a French citizen: not only those born in France or foreigners resident in France for one year or more, but, specifically, all of those whom the *legislative body* deems worthy of citizenship. There is a perfect *reflexive* circularity, then, between the singular and the universal. For this reason it does not yet attain the perspective of the *judgment of necessity* that exhibits the connection that, in the singular, binds the universal with the particular, the generic with the specific (as in the case of a federal state or, as in Spain, one that consists in autonomous regions). For the judgment of necessity expresses "the *universality that exists in and for itself* or *the objective universality* that in the sphere of essence corresponds to *substantiality*" (*WdL. GW* 12, 77; Di Giovanni, 575). In political terms this corresponds to the State as ethical substance (in the same way that the judgment of reflection *took up*, at the level of the concept, the absolute necessity of the "blind destiny" and the *abstract* revolutionary State at the political level).

For Hegel, as for Kant, the task is ultimately that of *learning* from the French Revolution, from its collapse into Terror, and subsequently from its *false* and abstract bourgeois renewal in the *July* Revolution of 1830, from the Empire and from the Restoration of the Ancien Régime. Learning from this *necessity* leads to the true resolution: the *Gemeinschaft* of the State, which in turn culminates in the *Gemeinde* and the establishment of a politics capable of reintroducing the singular will and the abstract will of the universal into the concrete universal will of a genuine ethical community. This would be the *Mitte* or heart that mediates between the objectivity of an "externally real" freedom and the subjectivity of an "internally formal" freedom. Such mediation finds expression in the *Verfassung* (not a mere *Konstitution* or *Charter* that is simply decreed from above), namely the constitution of an ethical life in which every individual can come together in accordance with his particular characteristics within the community, thereby establishing a national consensus that reflects at the level of objective spirit the religious core and heart of absolute spirit.

A final twist, moving at once beyond Hegel and with Hegel: this reflection of absolute spirit cannot be realized by any merely *internal* religiousness, or something felt merely in the private sphere. If heaven once came down to earth, though for a time it turned the latter into an inferno, this means there is no *ascension* here. Nor, on the other side, can this reflection be realized by any democracy that is merely formal, external, and quantitative in character, if it is certain that the Spirit dwells among us, and that its own (at least the Hegelians) have recognized it as such. At least, that is, in thought.

And then comes the know-it-all, *der Besserwissende*, to accuse Hegel on account of the witticism "so much the worse for the facts," and to remind us that neither the *Gemeinschaft* nor the *Gemeinde* have arrived, that we must therefore resign ourselves to what is the case, to the present, to the facts. What that basically amounts to is this: to assign the deceased to his place in imperious fashion and thus assume a position above and beyond him. And yet, as Adorno perceptively points out (I began with him and here I shall end with him), what we should be trying to learn is "what the present means in the eyes of Hegel."[60]

Or to put this in another way, if I may be permitted the harmless vanity of quoting myself, of learning "whether the claim to truth which his philosophy harbours still remains in force." This is what I wrote thirty-eight years ago,[61] having just emerged, not without certain wounds that have never fully healed, from the student troubles of May 1968. And I continue to think the same today. I continue to think with Aristotle that we can only speak the truth together, between all of us. I continue to think that it is solely the demand raised by truth that can save us from this circling combination of fire and water that culminates in terror and nihilism. It is only the quest for truth, undertaken together and with sacrifice, that can save us, and not the passive reception of a truth that is delivered from the rigid point of any ruling head that chooses a gulp of water with the taste of blood.

I continue to believe, in the end, in the words of the poet:

> "Your truth? No, the truth.
> Come and seek it with me.
> As for ours, keep it."[62]

Chapter IV

Person, Freedom, and Community

1. The Entire Remnant of the Idea

The last chapter of Hegel's *Science of Logic* opens with a paragraph that is as proud and confident in its movement as it is enigmatic in its content. At the boundaries of thought, the endeavors of the *vita activa* and the *vita contemplativa* are brought together to give birth to the absolute Idea. For the synthesis of these endeavors, of the theoretical and the practical, the Idea ceases to be "a sought for beyond and an unattained end" (*WdL. GW* 12, 236, line 5; Di Giovanni, 735). There is no longer any "beyond" (*Jenseits*): the absolute Idea is itself the limit of any thinking that encompasses all knowledge and all doing. It is a limit that gathers its own otherness within its infinite relation to itself, and turns that otherness into an evanescent moment: it is the positing of its own presupposition. Being the ground of the movement through which the Idea emerges as result, the Idea is thus itself the truth of its presupposition. That is why, on the one hand, it is a "return to life" (*WdL. GW* 12, 236, lines 10–11; Di Giovanni, 735). On the other hand, however, it is a pure positing of itself. In other words, it is something like an "implosion" of all its possible predicates, the mirroring inhesion of its own subsuming. It is therefore the "free subjective concept that exists for itself and therefore has *personality*" (*WdL. GW*, 236, line 13; Di Giovanni, 735). Hegel is quick to make the above qualification, for we might otherwise be misled into thinking that "personality" is a predicate of the "Idea"—as the subject, a predicate that could correspond to many others, while the subject could admit of other predicates as well. The rational concept, insofar as it is *omnimode determinatum*, coincides entirely with the *determining* predicate. It is thus "the practical objective Concept that is determined in and for itself and is as person impenetrable, atomic subjectivity" (*WdL. GW* 12, 236, lines 14–15; Di Giovanni, 735). It is therefore a sheer incommunicable punctuality. Yet this infinitively intense and concentrated subjectivity does not exclude anything from itself. There is nothing that could be opposed to it, either by being indifferent toward it or by confronting it. It is the sheer point of the non-difference or indifference (*Indifferenz*) of any determination. Beyond it there is no Other: all that is Other lies within and beneath it: "in its other it has *its own* objectivity for its object" (*WdL. GW* 12, 236, lines 16–17; Di Giovanni, 735).

And yet, suddenly and rather disconcertingly, Hegel concludes that "All the rest [*Alles Übrige*] is error, confusion, opinion, striving, arbitrariness, and transitoriness" (*WdL. GW* 12, 236, lines 17–18; Di Giovanni, 735). How can there remain anything else, anything left over that would exceed the absolute Idea? Is it not everything explained, everything reconciled in the Idea? Everything—for the determinations of thought that have been expounded in the *Logic*, and any possible word or thought that presupposes those pure essentialities, are now the *remains of the Logical*, its waste or *Abfall*. Everything, then, is reconciled with its own determination, vocation, or destiny (*Bestimmung*). From this pinnacle of the absolute Idea the determinations, in and for themselves, are recognized as confusion, arbitrariness, and transitoriness. And the Idea consists in and is exhausted in being the determinate negation of the pretensions to truth of each of those determinations (and a fortiori of any word with any meaning). In the face of these "remains" or this *Abfall*, the "absolute Idea *alone* is being, imperishable life, self-knowing truth, and is all truth" (*WdL. GW* 12, 236, lines 19–20; Di Giovanni, 735).

These are strange assertions: the thought of the infinite Person does not exclude anything, has nothing outside of itself. Thus what remains is *its* remains: the excess, its own excess. It is not so much that it is excessive, as that it is itself excess. Since it has nothing to reach for beyond itself, or anything by which it may be repelled, it is itself its own "beyond." The person *posits* its own remnant beyond itself, a remnant that is everything: the universe of discourse. The person (or more precisely, the Idea of the Person as atomic and impenetrable subjectivity) posits its own beyond. The unspeakable word in which all words are gathered, it is externality or "utterance" (*Äusserung*), a voice that hears itself, as Hegel says, but "one that in being externally uttered has immediately vanished again" (*WdL. GW* 12, 237, line 8; Di Giovanni, 736). It hears or apprehends its own difference (Hegel is playing here on the etymology of the German word for "reason" (*Vernunft*)—which is related to the idea of "hearing" or "perceiving": *vernehmen, per-cipere*—just as Jacobi did before him and Heidegger will do after him). Yet that difference, Hegel writes, "is not yet [*noch*] otherness [*Andersseyn*]" (*WdL. GW* 12, 237, line 10; Di Giovanni, 736). What is this "not yet"? In what sense can the irruption of a *temporal* adverb within the *Logic* be permitted? Only if we admit that the Idea, the original Word, is the promise of itself as the other of itself. Within the realm of Science the determinations are, for the Idea, *its* other, but not Otherness. Yet in that case the Idea fails to take its own determination and destiny with fully radical and *mortal* seriousness: if those determinations were exclusively intralogical, they would only *apparently* be errors (*errancy*), confusion, arbitrariness, and transitoriness. In the end, they would have been errors only for us, for us human beings, insofar as we take them as genuinely true expressions. But if the true is the Whole (that is: not "all" the determinations of thought, but precisely the energetic singleness of their negation), then nothing sayable or thinkable is, in and for itself, true, but rather at most "truthful" (*wahrhaftig*, rather than *wahr*).

This is, in my view, the great paradox of Hegel's *Logic*: not only do the expressions in which its exposition (*Darstellung*) consists increasingly develop and "mature," thereby changing their meaning in accordance with their different contexts, but it must also be recognized that they cannot simply be exclusively logical in character: they are already "judged" and "condemned" beforehand to be their own "otherness" or *Andersseyn*, and thus to differ from themselves, and not only from the other elements that form the entire logical structure. And a fortiori: the absolute Idea itself, which gathers all those determinations into itself by negating them, *eo ipso* "judges and condemns" itself to be its own *remains*, its own beyond. For this reason we must not say that the Idea *comes to be* nature, or passes over into nature, but rather that (in a true extra-logical *petitio principii*) it *re-leases* (*sich entläßt*) itself as nature, or freely lets itself go into and as nature.¹ That which was in and for itself the impenetrable and the atomic—the absolute Idea—releases itself as penetrability and continuity as such (*partes extra partes*). The sheer and internalized being-for-itself makes itself into the otherness of itself; not only exteriority but also being-outside-of-itself (*Aussersichseyn*). Not something apart from thought, but something refractory and impotent in the face of the concept.

Now this absolute that exits from itself harbors, in advance, the promise of reconstitution, of redemption, and that on account of a strict and expressly logical necessity. In effect, this errant path that Nature is, does not belong to her: it is not the errant path *of* nature (as a subjective genitive) but that *of* the Idea. Just as all logical determinations atoned for the *hubris* of regarding themselves as true in an unqualified sense, acquiring structure solely in the context of infinite negation, so too the natural determinations must internalize (*sich erinnern*) their own origin and recognize themselves, at last, for what they are: the logical power of negation is *their* own negation and therefore they will end up articulating a world, a complete and rational order that (for it could not be otherwise) consists of elements that for their part are really and "truthfully" confusion, arbitrariness, and transitoriness. Thus at the end of the path traced in the *Encyclopaedia* we discover the Idea that has "released itself" as an infinite return to itself: that rather strange and disquieting form of being that Hegel calls Absolute Spirit (or "God" in the figurative and representational language of religion) and that will maintain and preserve itself, as infinite Person and being-for-itself, in its Otherness, that is, in the world as *its* own objectivity. A world that will be, once more, and forever, errancy, arbitrariness, and transitoriness. To know oneself as *omnitudo negationum*: that is the word, almost sarcastic as it seems, for the only possible reconciliation, the only possible redemption, there is. This is the thought that everything is condemned to pass away and perish because, while constitutive of Spirit by virtue of its intrinsic contradiction, it does not constitute Spirit itself, though it cannot, by definition, exist outside or apart from Spirit either. If Spirit were flame, everything would be material for this conflagration, with nothing left over. And the Word in which all words are said, while it prevents any word from being intelligible solely by itself, turns into the Person for whom all things are ultimately appropriated as the one and only "Matter" or "Thing" (*Sache*), while those things (*Dinge*), for their part, are wholly consumed in this relationship. Yet if it is true that "The *weaker* can only be seized and invaded by the *stronger* in so far as it accepts the stronger and constitutes one *sphere* with it" (*WdL.* GW 12,140, lines 31–32; Di Giovanni, 638), then what is appropriated must grow in strength and cohesion, and let us say in refractoriness, until it is worthy of constituting that single sphere (the sphere of the "appropriating event," of *Ereignis*, to express it in Heideggerian terms) with the One who or That which appropriates (in the same way that the determinations of thought came increasingly to condense or concentrate their own meaning until they eventually constituted the very apex of the Idea, co-inciding in it without ever being simply identified with it. In a word, albeit a figurative or representational one: the sacrifice of actual reality for the sake of Spirit cannot limit itself to being the (self-)destruction of the physical, of intra-worldly things, but must rather involve the death of those who, being also persons, are able to release themselves—when their time comes—into their own beyond, turning themselves, in and through this process, into spirit too.

For a God who affirms himself in and as the destruction of all that exists, the only really appropriate offering is the free and conscious offering of one's own life. Of the life of free persons, offered up for the sake of the survival (always limited and precarious) of other free persons and, through them, of the Infinite Person: Spirit. Only such sacrificial death lives up to the demands of the Absolute Lord: Death itself, which preserves and maintains itself as infinite Life precisely in and through the deaths of human beings: in the ab-negation of the latter in order that the eternal Death of death may be eternally fulfilled, in order that that "Once" (the once-upon-a-time when the God who became man died, returning to the Past in which He always was) may be "Always" (*einmal ist allemal*). This is Hegelian philosophy: a kind of Platonizing *praeparatio mortis* but one more fearsomely and monstrously radical than that so eloquently apostrophized by Plato in the *Phaedo*. It is more radical because, while negating of course the hope of the individual, it transfigures that hopelessness and that despair into a vast project of the socioreligious realization of the Kingdom of God on Earth (following in the footsteps of Pelagius, Joachim da Fiore, and Lessing). And this is because for Hegel the conscious awareness of human mortality is the only reliable guarantee of the persistence of the human Community. Death, the "beyond" of the person, is the time of freedom within the Community. This is the view I will now try to develop.

2. Person as a Relational Nature

The term "person," reflecting a core idea that still echoes the classical definition of Boethius,[2] comes to acquire an ever-richer meaning as its referent becomes itself more complex over time. Its initial logical configuration in Hegel is that of *being-for-itself*; the posited identity of the being-within-itself (*Insichseyn*) and the *limit (Grenze)*; being-for-itself is "*das sich auf sich beziehende Negative, das absolute Bestimmtseyn*: the negative which relates to itself, the absolutely determined being" (*WdL. GW* 11, 86, lines 10–11). What characterizes this category or determination of being is that otherness and community with another have been sublated as a moment within this very being-for-itself (86, lines 26–28). In relating to another, it relates to something sublated: it is only reflected into itself in negating the other, which now appears without independence or as a mere "being-for-another" (87, lines 22–30). From here we can easily trace the characteristics, already familiar in the philosophical tradition, of the "impenetrability" and "individuality" of personality, and especially its absolutely *relational* nature: its being is a self-relation in terms of the negativity of what is other than itself.[3]

Person is thus individual (atomic) and incommunicable (impenetrable) being-for-itself insofar as it posits itself in the negation of all independent or "autonomous" otherness. This makes its first phenomenological appearance in the well-known dialectic of master and slave. There Hegel tells us: "The individual who has not risked his life may well be recognized as a *person*, but he has not attained to the truth of this recognition as an independent self-consciousness" (*Phä.* IV, A; *GW* 9, 111, lines 34–36; Miller, 114). He can in effect be recognized as a person from the moment in which the slave, *as worker*, negates the autonomy or independent otherness of matter, negating at the same time the satisfaction of his own desire: it is his own negative relation to the object that gives form to the latter. In himself, or for us, the slave is therefore already a person, but not a person *for himself* since that double negation came about only out of the fear of the Absolute Lord, that is, the fear of Death. His recognition has been bestowed rather than acquired. Yet the master cannot consider himself a person either: if indeed, on the one hand, he risks his life (i.e., puts at stake the essence that constitutes him), he still depends, on the other hand, on two forms of otherness: in an immediate fashion on the labor of the slave, in a mediated fashion on the external nature that he enjoys only through that labor. We can only meaningfully speak of a "person" when autonomy (the truth of self-certainty) and the negation of externality (through property and labor) come together in one and the same subject.

It is in the Roman world of legal status (*Rechtzustand*) that the person, strictly speaking, makes its appearance as spirit. There where the *res publica* (*Gemeinwesen*: *Phä. GW* 9, 260, line 27), as the unconscious substance of individuals, has been lost, the universal breaks up "into the atoms of the absolute plurality of individuals" (*Phä. GW* 9, 260, line 30; Miller, 290). Here they all count *equally*: each represents the totality with the same right. The fact that each one recognizes the other in this *abstract universality* that is contradictory and doomed to conflict (everyone is "I" and thus the affirmation of such selfhood on the part of the other excludes him from my selfhood), now constitutes *substantiality*, the single "common essence." Thus they all coincide in being, with an equal right, distinguishable from one another and precisely for that reason indistinguishable with respect to themselves: they are individuals and atoms. First nature, or sensuous externality, has been negated through property and work; and second nature, the ethical life of the *polis*, has been negated through the abstract and empty character of a universal *res publica* (*Gemeinwesen*), although it is universal only through the forcible exclusion of all difference and distinction. In reality the person, as a term of reflection, simply reflects within itself the vacuity of that *res publica*.

The dialectic that "the person" must undergo proves devastating for its claim to unite singularity and universality within itself through the negation of all distinction: the self-consciousness that can make itself valued and recognized as something effectively autonomous does indeed discover the full freedom of its spirit here. Yet this remains a *libertas indifferentiae*, an inessential form of action that cannot fix its desire on anything without the risk of reifying itself, of losing its freedom. It is true that what is actual, insofar as I appropriate it and the others recognize this as my property, is *mine* (*Phä. GW* 9, 262, line 18; Miller, 292). But this "mine"—something that has validity inasmuch as it is juridically acknowledged—has no effect either on the pure vacuity of my Self (which cannot *com-mit* me to anything and thus expose me to what is arbitrary or contingent) or on the Matter or Thing Itself that is what it is independently of whether it belongs to me or not. In the experience of *abstract right*, what the acquisitive consciousness attains is precisely the *loss* of its own reality: it is not itself, as it had believed, but rather the vacuous reflection of the empty universal *res publica* (in which "everyone" is "each one"), so that their common essence is in fact inessentiality (*Unwesentlichkeit*). Hegel's conclusion here is succinct: "to describe an individual as a 'person' is an expression of contempt" (*Phä. GW* 9, 262, line 27; Miller, 292). These words undoubtedly echo the old etymology of "person" as mask (*persona* in Latin or *prosopon* in Greek).[4] Behind the mask there is nothing but sheer negativity: the content, the substantiality has been negated only in an abstract way (it is Nature as the Non-I). Thus in the negative and infinite self-relation of the person that content has been detached, set loose, and exposed to the rapacity of whichever person arbitrarily appropriates that content and establishes himself as the "lord of the world" (*Herr der Welt*; 9: 263, line 13; Miller, 293—the Imperator, the spiritual shape of the Master from the *Phenomenology*). And this single One confronts all other persons as a devastating and destructive power. Yet this supreme Person does not cease, in the end, to be a person. In other words: he is "the formal self" (*das formelle Selbst*) (*Phä. GW* 99, 263, line 11; Miller, 293), who in acting in a merely capricious way is actually subjected to the capriciousness of external nature. He is *outside of himself*, just as nature itself is, and is thus in truth the agent who reintroduces the Absolute Lord as that Death that in principle had been postponed and repressed through the work of the slave. It is quite true that the Lord of the World, the absolute yet abstract person, is "conscious of its complete supremacy" (*Phä. GW* 99, 263, line 27; Miller, 293), and "thinks of itself as being an actual living God" (*Phä. GW* 99, 263, line 10; Miller, 293). Yet this supremacy or omnipotence is an illusory one; in and for itself this God is just the incapacity, in the barren purity of his negative individuality, to overcome the dispersed exteriority of what is alien to and other than himself. He is, therefore, a posited contradiction, along with the persons he dominates (who at any time might also "represent," by a stroke of luck, the "persona" of Lord of the World). This is the contradiction: it is "the universal actuality of the self; but this actuality is directly the perversion [or 'inversion,' *Verkehrung*; in Greek: 'katastrophē'—F.D.] of the self as well. It is the loss of its essence" (*Phä. GW* 99, 264, lines 2–3; Miller, 293–94). The person is thus the spirit which is alienated from itself (*sich entfremdet*).

Yet in spite of the negative connotations of the concept of "person," Hegel will never abandon this moment in which substance has become subject or individual. As we know, the highest and ultimate logical determination, the one in which all thought is gathered, is described as "person," just as the Supreme Being, or Absolute Spirit, will reveal itself as the relation of three Persons who are identical in their difference from one another. With the "person" the ancient ethical substance of the Greek world has achieved consciousness of itself, thereby establishing freedom and equality, albeit in an initially abstract way. The question now is precisely that of overcoming this abstraction, of acquiring truly concrete form. The required concretion is attained in a twofold process: through free interpersonal recognition and through the determinate negation of all alien externality, namely of nature. These are two parallel processes that will come together and be consummated in what we may call the "extra-position" of full and concrete Personality (Spirit) in and as its own Beyond or *Jenseits*: in the Christian community or *Gemeinde*. Yet to attain that consummation—where the free logical self-releasement of the Idea in and as Nature is accomplished and fulfilled, thus completing in flesh and blood what initially was merely the "divine concept" (*WdL. GW* 12, 253, lines 4–5)—we shall have to traverse, with Hegel, the arid desert of "abstract right" and the profoundly troubled and self-destructive world of "civil society." This is our desert, our world.

3. Abstract Right and Legal Recognition

In Abstract Right, the mask or character becomes a real person from the moment in which the individual attains *legal* recognition on the part of others of his existence as owner. The foundation and historical genesis of Right lies in Rome, but its real existence, its establishment as universal law, has only been accomplished in the modern world in terms of a double determination: (1) *the freedom of the person*, which is intrinsically demanded by Christianity and which puts an end to slavery (*de iure* if not *de facto*), thus establishing the equality of all human beings *qua* subjects; and (2) the *freedom of property* that was established by the French Revolution.[5] These two phenomena are separated from one another by more than 1,500 years, but are nonetheless strictly connected from the systematic and philosophical point of view. It is here, in Abstract Right, that the "person" is precisely to be located from the systematic perspective of the *Encyclopaedia*. And it is from here, whether by defect or excess, that the abstract person of the *cives romanus* or the divine Person of Christianity analogically derive. This is Hegel's definition: "The freedom which we have here is what is called a person, i.e. the subject who is free, free indeed for himself [*für sich*], and who gives himself an existence [*Dasein*] in things [*Sachen*]" (*Rechtsphil.* §33, *Zusatz*, 69; Knox, 52). Here we can immediately see the intimate contradiction in the concept of "person." Being free, that is, withdrawn and set loose from natural and factical things (*Dinge*), the subject knows itself as negative infinitude: pure being-for-itself. But that infinitude is wholly empty: the person can become anything or something (*Sache*) because of itself—it is not determinate or determined in any way at all; or rather, the person is determined precisely by not being anything finite, or anything qualitatively defined. But then the existence that the person gives to him- or herself is wholly contingent and arbitrary: "A person has the right of putting his will into any and every thing [*Sache*] and thereby making it *mine*, turning it into my substantial end because it has no such end in itself" (*Rechtsphil*. §44, 79; Knox, 60—English translation modified). It is true, on the one hand, that this way of proceeding and this right demonstrate the inconstancy and lack of inner reality of supposedly external things. This is the negation and undoing of the thing that renders it insubstantial. On the other hand, however, the person enjoys no existence outside of the thing that has been possessed: for that particular existence itself negates, ipso facto, the supposed negative universality of freedom. With this bond to something material (however humanized the latter has become) the subject finds itself forced to recognize that if, on the one hand, the Thing is subjected to him as his property, then he himself, on the other hand, is subjected to the Thing insofar as he is subject *to* needs and necessities (*Bedürfnisse*). Such an inversion of subjection is, however, entirely leveled out quantitatively when the things are compared among themselves with regard to their utility, and thus with regard to the needs that they fulfill. Things and needs thus become interchangeable: they all acquire an exchange value, the universal measure of which is money (*Rechtsphil*. §63, 96ff.; Knox, 74–75). The thing, initially bare and immediate, then worked on and developed, and finally a pure object of designation, is now turned into a *sign*, the solid basis and guarantee for the production of *contracts*: the mutual recognition of persons mediated through a domesticated nature, a nature that has been volatized to the point of becoming a mere quantitative and homogeneous substrate. The person of Abstract Right has thus posited its own "beyond": the community (*Gemeinschaft*) of goods, the object of contract. But then, in this case, the person neither entirely fulfills the logical potentialities that are harbored within his own definition, nor is such a "beyond," this *second nature*, capable of restoring in a reflected fashion the infinite force of free subjectivity. On the contrary, the double dialectic of the juridical person and of the contractual community necessarily leads to the inversion of this sphere: right or law turns into wrong or lawlessness (*Unrecht*), into deception and crime. And it necessarily leads to this because juridical equality (the level of the free will) has natural inequality as its correlate (the level of characteristics and properties whose possession in some cases creates privation in others).

However, and most significantly, it is precisely in transgression, and the punishment that corresponds to it, that the person achieves real (and no longer merely formal) freedom, while the community ceases to be a merely contractual association in order to become rational. Thus a kind of double elevation takes place here. On the one hand, it is the reflection on the deed that has been committed, a reflection occasioned by the punishment imposed by the judge (a singular person who is nonetheless disinterested or impartial, and who is thus the one who guarantees the universality of Law), which brings the criminal to *interiorize* the law that has been infringed. It is precisely in this way that the moral subject is born. On the other hand, that reflection is accomplished in light of the general accountability or imputability that is presupposed by the community. Thus, in making the person into a "responsible" subject, this community itself acquires the status of *ethical substance*. The first aspect, in which the interiorized personality is central, will form the sphere of morality, while the second one, in which the community as substance assumes priority, will constitute the sphere of *Sittlichkeit* or the ethical life (in an inverse parallelism with the double movement of the Absolute Idea, which was, on the one hand, a "return to life"—to ethical life—and on the other, a free non exclusive person).

Yet before we can attain that logical-religious summit it is necessary to traverse the region of despair: the *system of needs*. And it is only by means of this system—since it is the middle (*Mitte*), that is, the negative term of ethical life—that *man* (properly speaking) and *society* alike arise through the harsh recognition of need

(*Bedürfnis*). In the context of Abstract Right this need was a mere appearance: nature seemed to be *formally* reduced to the universal field of what is ready to hand. But in the civil society need makes its real appearance (*Erscheinung*). In the earlier ethical stage, that is, that of the family, needs were met in the circle of feminine *pietas*: the acknowledgement of the latter as trusting love found expression as religion. But this was an unconscious and natural religion, not the religion of free human beings. In the realm of work and business there is no place for this comforting refuge: for there "faith, simple customs, and the religious dimension all vanish" (*Rechtsphil. Anhang zu* §182, 474; not included in Knox). Only within the void of that disappearance does the *universality of thought* emerge for the individual. The terrible and brutal difference between those who possess the means of production (a possession not only of Things but of the means and methods for producing and multiplying things) and those who only possess their own bodies (labor power) but not the outcome of their externalizing activity, and even those *misérables* who cannot alienate that activity (the rabble or *Pöbel*): paradoxically enough, it is this unbearable difference that at the same time will generate the ethical-political ideal of a reconciled Humanity.

Hegel does not delude himself with false hope here. With an astonishing coldness (far from Feuerbach's sentimentality or from a certain kind of messianic or eschatological Marxism), the German thinker here exposes the contradiction of civil society, a contradiction that is irresolvable from within that sphere. On the one hand, thanks to the system of needs, Hegel says: "Man *qua* man, thus as particular individual, has to come into existence, must become truly actual; this is inherent in the right of subjective freedom . . . here is where anyone can pursue what he sees as his calling" (*Rechtsphil. Anhang zu* §200, 486; not included in Knox). Yet on the other hand, that calling is obstructed (for all human beings, not only for the worker) because the tendency toward the division of labor, of the means of production, and of goods, brings about the uniformity and standardization of everything, a process accelerated by the emergence of *mechanization*. The machine, in the end: "makes man superfluous" (*Rechtsphil. Anhang zu* §198, 485; not included in Knox).

This should not be misunderstood: it is not a question of some empirically existing inequality, one that could be solved through the better distribution of wealth or the collective participation in the ownership of the means of production (a participation that, for Hegel, would literally be "catastrophic"—an inversion of the order articulated in the *Encyclopaedia*—for it would mean turning the State into a kind of juridical macro-personality). No, the system of needs (without any consoling utopias) is inevitably bound up with the "state of necessity" (*Notstaat*): its fundamental class, the *Fabrikantenstand* (*Rechtsphil. Anhang zu* §204, 487; not included in Knox), is essentially characterized by its boundless greed and insatiability with regard to the accumulation of goods. And this not for the sake of the goods themselves; the deep reason for this overwhelming reemergence of the person at the heart of civil society, as Veblen puts it, "is the desire of everyone to excel everyone else in the accumulation of goods[. . . .] Since the struggle is substantially a race for reputability, [. . .] no approach to a definitive attainment is possible."[6]

This is, indeed, an unbridled and exorbitant race to attain reputation. Here, once again, man achieves the opposite of what he is seeking. He would like to be more than anyone else, to be the One and Only One: but this supposed uniqueness is based on recognition from others; yet this is not a recognition of the person (in that regard we are all the same), but of the man who, having the capacity to satisfy all his needs, thus feels continually compelled to invent new "needs," which are not and cannot be shared, precisely in order to *distinguish himself* from others. And this, in turn, provokes both admiration and bitterness in others. For the *beati possidentes*, in the end, depend on the infinite particularity into which nature, self-external as it is, breaks open. Far from being a free and negatively assumed infinitude, they find themselves delivered over to the opinion of others and to the opacity of what is other: this is the highest alienation. In civil society, wealth is not enjoyed: it is displayed. In the end it is merely self-display. Sheer glitter, insubstantial semblance (*Schein*): the state of necessity (*Notstaat*) is the state of Nature (*Naturstaat*).

4. Ethical Life and Bourgeois Virtues

There is no way back. It would be useless to preach the virtues of chastity, poverty, and obedience. It would be useless and also undesirable. For ethical life is built on contrary virtues: marriage, the acquisition of goods through labor, the observance of the universal: observance of the Law, but not of the Lord (whether it be the extramundane Lord or the Lord of the World) (cf. *Enz.* §552, *Anm.*; *W.* 10, 358f.; Wallace, 286 f.). But this last point involves the preservation of ethical life by and within the State: *die Sittlichkeit im Staate*. And Hegel adds: "*so kann dann erst Recht und Moralität vorhanden sein*" ("Thus, and thus only, can law and morality exist") (ibid.; Wallace, 286). This precise point has a very far-reaching significance: right (the kingdom of persons and their property) and morality (the inner kingdom of subjects and their obligations) are abstractions from that rational substance which is the State. This latter is what preserves and maintains those spheres. But to preserve them does not mean to cancel their deficiencies: the state lives from the very regulation of those deficiencies. Furthermore, the state itself is doomed to pass over to the other of itself, to its "beyond." It does not redeem the citizens from their condition as persons. On the contrary: it guarantees and perpetuates that condition: "Private citizens are in the state the incomparably greater number (*Menge*) and form the multitude of such as are recognized as persons" (*Enz.* §544, *A.*; *W.* 10, 343; Wallace, 273). It was the State that formed the foundation of the rational community that acknowledged imputability, that acknowledged persons as free and responsible for their actions.

Yet by whom will the State itself be judged? On the one hand, the supreme Person in the state, the monarch (who represents the role of "princely coercion") also possesses the characteristics of the person, and this in the highest degree: "The I [. . .] is at once the most individual and the most universal" (*Rechtsphil.* §275, *Zusatz*, 319; Knox, 264, translation slightly adapted). Thus, as Hegel writes: "It is only as a *person*, the *monarch*, that the personality of the state is actual" (*Rechtsphil.* §279, 323; Knox, 267). But that person is, by origin, purely natural. His status depends on the contingent circumstances of birth, thereby producing a violent conjunction in which both the highest and the lowest are united without any possible synthesis or harmony: "*this* individual is raised to the dignity of monarchy in an immediate, natural, fashion, that is, through his *natural* birth [*Geburt*]" (*Rechtsphil.* §280, 327; Knox, 271). And it could not be otherwise: for Hegel (contrary to the nonsensical accusations of political accommodation and opportunism), neither the individuals of civil society (the bourgeoisie) nor persons in the juridical sense could freely elect their own representatives without inverting the order articulated in the *Encyclopaedia*. It is the "I" of the monarch, the pure and free will, that originates and provides the condition of possibility for the citizen to be able to designate himself as an "I." Yet that supreme I, as we saw before, depends in itself (not in its function, not as a "personage") on what can never be an "I": on the blind and amorphous causality of nature.

The same thing happens with regard to the State itself. Regarded as an individual whole (the Nation as single and indivisible Nation), the state is exposed to externality, is necessarily cast out into nature: it "appears in immediate actuality as a *single* nation [*einzeln*: "one among many"] that is *naturally* determined" (*Enz.* §545; *W.* 10, 345; Wallace, 275). In this regard nations reproduce, at a global level, the war of all against all that is characteristic of civil society. Once again, we see how the maximum punctuality, the purest negative self-relation to itself, is split in and as its own "beyond": the model of the self-release of the Idea in and as Nature ominously and inexorably governs the evolution of the person throughout the realm of objective spirit. And it does so implacably and irreversibly.

Is Hegel, then, the Emperor of thought? That may well be so. But we must recognize, with Hegel, that all *imperium* is destined to failure. And so too the supreme *Imperium*: that of the threefold divine personality.

Hegelian religion is not that of a blessed *identitas in Uno*, a happy and innocent life in common where contention would be unknown (like some innocuous *communio sanctorum*) precisely because, in the end, everything *would be the same*, would be indifferent in the eyes of the omnipotent Lord. Quite the contrary: "The aim of philosophy is to banish indifference and come to know the necessity of things so that the other is seen to stand over against [*gegenüberstehend*] *its* other" (*Enz.* §119, Z. 1; *W.* 8, 246; Wallace, 174). This also holds for God, especially for God. He is at once a supreme struggle and a conciliation, not indeed a conciliation *of* this struggle but *within* this struggle. Hegelian religion is not the Greek religion of *fate*, but nor is it one of *consolation*. The latter is peculiar to modern man who, whenever he fails to attain his subjective aims and finds himself obliged to give up hope, "consoles himself with the prospect of receiving compensation [*Ersatz*] in some other form" (*Enz.* §147, Z.; *W.* 8, 291; *Hegel's Logic*, Wallace, 209–10). And, according to Hegel, it is the Christian God himself who teaches us, as free personalities, to stand beyond despair, but also indeed beyond hope (a virtue that is conspicuously absent from the encyclopedic system). Thus Hegel writes: "If a man saw, on the contrary, that whatever happens to him is only the outcome of himself, and he only bears his own guilt [*Schuld*], he would stand free, and in everything that came upon him would have the consciousness that he suffered no wrong" (*W.* 8, 292; *Hegel's Logic*, Wallace, 211). And that is due to the fact that "God is not only known merely [by the community, F.D.] but also self-knowing; he is a personality not merely figured or represented in our minds [that is, a *person* in the Latin sense of the term: only a 'personage' or 'representative'—F.D.], but rather absolutely actual personality" (ibid.).

As soon as that personality is absolute, it cannot be "outside of itself," nor can it *pass over* to its other. There is nothing outside: God himself sees himself as his own other, an other that is now interior to himself. That other is, once again and for the last time, "nature": but no longer the external nature in which the absolute Idea poured itself, but a personalized and spiritualized nature: the community of the faithful, the Christian *Gemeinde*. And shall we, at last, find *peace* here? Will all those contradictions now be finally resolved—crime at the heart of the state under the rule of law, the intolerable inequality of goods within civil society, war among the States at the global level? Absolutely not: the lowest form of religiosity (corresponding to the lowest estate of society: the productive class) is the religiosity of the *heart* (the *inner* reemergence of the person who fatuously believes himself to be the only depositary of truth).

And this necessarily leads to the corruption of the Church. The middle sphere, characteristic of Modernity and the Enlightenment, falls apart into two extreme forms of representational thought that are both equally vacuous: on the side of abstract intellectualism, and in the name of Universal Freedom, we find an a priori condemnation of any individual spirit for being already a potential "suspect," thus producing a form of slavery that is more dreadful than that of the Roman person before the Lord of the World (it is possible, at least, to rise up against *this* man, the Imperator, yet who would rise up against the System, against the *Être suprême*?); and on the side of pietism, in turn, we find that the beautiful souls of the faithful are essentially transformed into "abstract subjectivity, a subjectivism without any content" (*V-Rel.* 5, 267; Hodgson 3, 344).

The Christian community, torn apart by this polarity (two extremes that lead to the same vacuity), sinks and perishes. On the one hand, we have the scandal of a *people* who find their support in immediate faith, clinging to the sensible (as, for example, the *catholic* belief in the persisting presence of Christ and of blood in the consecrated Host, even when this is not consumed). On the other hand, we have an *enlightened* stratum that turns the life of spirit into a simulacrum, into a kind of pious *theatrical representation* (as, for example, the *Calvinist* belief in the Host as merely a symbol for something irretrievably past). It is true that the Lutheran believes in the *manducatio spiritualis*, the real presence of Christ at the very moment when the words of the ritual coincide with the actual consumption of the bread and wine, or in other words: with the *physical destruction* of something that is merely immediate, merely natural. But this presence of *Person to person*, of Spirit to spirit, is too reminiscent of the legal contract in which, as we saw earlier, people recognize one another via the middle term of the thing that is exchanged. What is exchanged here is an act of destruction; it is anticipation of the offering of one's own life: the past life of Christ, the future life of the believer. Yet who is capable, in the supreme sacramental moment, of living one's own *real* death, not the Jesuitical *simulacrum* of death or the Lutheran death within life, through the disappearance of individual freedom?

5. A Strange Sort of Redemption

"But when the fullness of the time was come, God sent forth his Son, born of a woman, born under the law."[7] Christ has gathered up the times in the one and only time, the time of the infinite freedom of the personality that accepts and interiorizes its twofold natural origin: the external one (Jesus is a man, born of a woman) and that of abstract substantiality (Jesus as begotten of the Father: the law that rises, in its transcendence, above every phenomenon). Now the spirit knows of its infinitude and its substantiality in one subject of immediate self-consciousness, in one infinite and *personal* negativity (*V-Rel.* 5, 80; Hodgson 3, 144). The logical, the *logos*, has transpired in the world, but as the world's negativity: as its own *lack*. But now, once again and for good, the times have not been fulfilled: rather, it is time itself that has been fulfilled, devoured in and through its own necessity (this is the supreme hyperbole, in terms of the relation between Spirit and its *Gemeinde*, of the "system of Needs": when "the teaching of this truth is no longer justified in terms of faith, once the time has come [or has been fulfilled—*erfüllet*] when what is demanded [or is the need: *Bedürfnis*] is justification by the concept" (*V-Rel.* 5, 95; Hodgson 3, 160–61). When History as *Geschichte* attempts to turn back on itself, to give an account of itself historiographically in terms of *Historie*, and thus falls victim the dead weight of the "thus it was" (something that Nietzsche too will denounce), then everything is finished: *consummatum est*, "*so ist es aus*."[8] This justification through the concept, in which religion finds *refuge* in philosophy, turns into a new and strange rational *community* (the figure of the end of times), although it is still isolated and misunderstood, the preserve of "an isolated order of priests" (*eine isolierte Priesterschaft*): yet, what can all this really mean? For it seems impossible to see how the general project of Hegelian philosophy, namely "the reconciliation of the self-conscious reason with the reason which is in the world—in other words with actuality" (*Enz.* §6; *W.* 8, 47; Wallace, 8) can be made compatible with the melancholic conclusion of the 1821 autograph manuscript: "we are untroubled about how it goes with the world . . . how things turn out in the world is not our affair" (*V-Rel.* 5, 97; Hodgson 3, 162).

But perhaps the solution is as painful as it is trivial, and it may already lie here within our grasp. Let us recall where we began: the consideration of the absolute Idea as pure Personality. Everything else, all that remains, was arbitrariness, confusion, and transitoriness. What are these "remains," then, but the entire Other of the Idea in which the latter now possesses its own objectivity? What is this "remnant" but the very transitoriness of the community, a transitoriness that does not pass away, that never ends, for it is only in that strangely *permanent* and constant transitoriness, in that mortality of the *Gemeinde*, that the Person of Spirit can recognize itself? What then "remains" for us, the members of that community, instructed as we are by that cold and lucid Hegelian "priesthood," but to recognize, in the premonition of the imminence of our own death, that we are only *really and truly* free when mutually recognizing our own necessary sins, or the sin of existing? To what is the *consummatum est* of the Cross a response? What is affirmed in the "reconciling *Yea*"?[9] Perhaps what is affirmed in that strange sort of *redemption* is nothing but the detachment of the "I" from its own ontic existence insofar as this existence is counterposed to that of the others, so as to configure that existence, in Hegel's words, as "the *existence* [*Dasein*] of the 'I' that has expanded into a duality [of the 'I,' then, that is shared and di-vided—F.D.], and therein remains identical with itself [the infinite doubling, the folding of Spirit, of the Supreme Person, in and as community—F.D.], and in its complete [consummated, *volkommenen*] externalization and opposite, possess the certainty of itself" (*Phä. GW* 9: 362, lines 26–28; Miller, 409). The mutual forgiveness of sins is the mutual abandonment of "I-hood": the definitive "beyond" of the person in the consummated time of the Community of free men, a time that does not pass because everything is already fulfilled, because now the truth of error, the necessity of chance and the eternity of transitoriness have been accepted. To live in the other, for the other, is to *die to ourselves*, in a truly *God-like* way: "It is God manifested in the midst of those who know themselves in the form of pure knowledge" (9: 362, lines 28–29; Miller, 409).

Where, O Death, is your victory? Death has been overcome, forever. But it has been overcome by the DEATH OF DEATH (*V-Rel*.5, 67; Hodgson 3, 131), by "dying to the natural" (*Absterben dem Natürlichen*) (*V-Rel*. 5, 64; Hodgson 3, 128; translation adapted). This is neither a utopian project nor a *pium desiderium*. With regard the private person, sentenced and destined to the realm of the natural, it is a *condemnation*: to be a Hegelian is to accept this condemnation, and do so freely and with full awareness.

Chapter V

The Errancy of Reason
(The Perishing of the Community)

> And all will have to die on account of you? asked Jesus. If you put the question like that, yes, all will die on account of me [. . .] it will be an endless history of blood and iron, of fire and ashes, an infinite sea of sufferings and tears. [. . .] One must be God, said the Devil, to be content with so much blood.
>
> —José Saramago, *O Evangelho Segundo Jesus Cristo*

1. The Devil, the Good Lord, and Human Blood

The Devil says, "One has to be God to be content with so much blood." Thus, on the one side, the Devil sees the contentment of God, and on the other the blood that is shed on account of human beings and at the hands of human beings. The Devil establishes, therefore, a negative infinite judgment. He emphatically upholds the unfathomable separation between God and man, and does so because he, the Demonic One, is incapable of sacrifice. He is no mortal. Being the spirit of all lies, being simply abstract negation, he is denied all *abnegation*. He does indeed say "No." But, unlike Antigone and Christ, he does so not to prepare himself for death, but in order to *negate death*. In this way he is, ab initio, spared the possibility of all communication, of all connection. He simply is exclusive singularity.

As pure egoism, he involves himself in nothing. It is the Devil, not God, who would constitute, for Hegel, the solar eye, as it were, of pure disinterested contemplation, for nothing transpires with the Devil. His power to tempt lies solely and entirely in this: to uphold in a fixed and rigid form the limits and distinctions between Idea, Nature, and Spirit—a purely lineal reading to accompany every meaningful claim or proposition without committing to or involving itself in any. It is thus by virtue of this liminal *innocence* that he can protest against the cruelty of God. For the Devil, it is God who must assume the blame, the burden, the charge, or the debt that his creatures bear since he has failed to furnish the measure for what they, fundamentally, are. God: this is the Excess by virtue of which all else is defective. Would it not have been better for God, and for all of us, if He were simply that, namely God, while human beings were simply that, namely human beings? This is the thinking of abstract negation: the frozen form of nothing. For God, then, would be [. . .] just God, and human beings [. . .] just human beings: a harmless repetition. Nothing.

Jesus says to the Scribes "Verily I say unto you, All sins shall be forgiven unto the sons of men, and blasphemies wherewith soever they shall blaspheme: But he that shall blaspheme against the Holy Spirit hath never forgiveness, but is in danger of eternal damnation."[1] This is how Jesus responds to the charge of being possessed by the Devil, and thus of being able to drive out demons or evil spirits. The Devil, the Demonic One, however, is incapable of turning against himself, for he is not indeed a Self (*Selbst*), but only a pure and conceited emptiness. He cannot be forgiven since, fundamentally, and beyond all popular images and representations of him, *he has never sinned*. In other words, he has never been fallen with respect to his rights. In its pure obstinacy, it would be a mistake to turn this figure into something like a personification of Nature, which, by contrast, is entirely full and level: the falling-away from itself, the de-cadence (*Abfall*), of the divine Idea.[2] If he were anything at all, the Devil would be God before all *de-cision*, before all resolve in virtue of which he could be at-home-with-himself (*bei-sich-selbst*) and, thereby, posit himself as present-to-and-over-against-himself (*gegen-wärtig*), as nature and as finite spirit. But God *is* this decision:

pure self-externalization or *kenōsis*. And if this is so, then the Devil is an impossible dream, a counterfactual condition: the unthinkable idea of a God who did not harbor within himself, as a necessary moment, his own death, namely the death of God in his abstract and immutable character.

Alien to the bloody shambles of history, the Devil is, then, a pure marginality: the dream of absolute innocence; like the spotless hands that need no washing since they have never incurred condemnation, since they have never become involved in the *ways* of worldly being. In his *Lectures on the Philosophy of Religion* Hegel alludes with searching depth to a passage in the Gospel of Mark: "*What is devoid of spirit [das Geistlose] is not sinful* except [when done] with a knowing and willing that is directed at the acknowledged spirit—it knows not spirit and thus is *innocent*. But this is *the innocence [Unschuld:* blamelessness, the absence of sin or trespass] that is judged and condemned precisely in itself."[3] Forgive us our trespasses—yet one who, *ab origine*, is without trespass or transgression can never be forgiven. Such "blamelessness" stands entirely this side of all reconciliation. There is no stain or defect, for no mark has been made. Unblemished, such a one can have no fate. For there is nowhere to go. This place can only be the desert. A place that annuls itself. Here one knows neither the pain of dissension nor the joy of reconciliation. Such a one is an unborn, a nothing. This is but an infinite nostalgia of impossibility: not to have been born, not to die. Captured by Midas, and compelled to abandon the *muteness that belongs to him*, to declare what would be the best for man, Silenus finally admitted: "For all, for all men and all women, the best is not to have been born. But, given this, the best that is granted to man, though second in worth to the former, is to die as soon as he has been born."[4]

And this is the right reply for a demon. To avoid suffering, and to avoid blood. Moreover, this is, *eo ipso*, to avoid acknowledgement of a lack or fault, of a distance: that which intervenes between the self-equality of the logical and the diversity of the natural. To impede this scission, this original doubling or bifurcation (*Entzweiung*), is to impede pain, and with that, to impede *life*. For "*pain* is the prerogative [*Vorrecht*: the primitive and original right] of living natures, since they are the concretely *existing* [*existierende*] concept."[5] And for this reason, if it is true that the Hegelian God, the Christian God, is the way (the path, the meaning), the truth, and *the life*, then this God is not lacking in pain or grief. On the contrary, he is the infinite grief, the infinite capacity to maintain and preserve himself in the midst of universal grief. The Maker of history is the difference between time as the Concept that is there (*da ist*: *Phä.*, *GW* 9, 429, line 7; Miller, 487) and the *end* or *purpose* (*Zweck*) as the Concept that exists (*existiert*),[6] that is, that freely arises in face of the Object and its process, precisely as its *fate* (*Schicksal*). This is why living beings, and preeminently human beings, are the Concept in its *Existenz*. And as such they are culpable, in debt to the origin in which they discover themselves, and of which they are custodians with regard to the *possibility* of the consummation, the fulfilment of that origin. In this connection there is a passage in Hegel's *Lectures on the Philosophy of Religion* that is particularly worthy of careful study and attention. Here Hegel claims that it is specifically characteristic of Christianity to have become aware of the unity between the divine nature and human nature. At first it might appear that man must be regarded as the virtual bearer (*an sich*) of the divine idea. But in what actually follows, Hegel corrects this impression (fortunately enough, for we only have to recall the well-known fascist slogan invented by José Antonio Primo de Rivera: "Man is a bearer of Eternal Values"—as if we were made to bear some kind of alien burden). For it is not that man would bear this Idea externally, but rather that the divine Idea is his own *substantial nature*, his vocation and innermost destination (*seine Bestimmung*). Hegel then says that man is the "unique possibility" of the Idea (*derselben*). In other words, this "infinite *possibility* is his own (*seine*) subjectivity."[7] What emerges here is an inversion of devastating consequences with regard to the traditional doctrine. In effect, we are being asked to think that, if the divine Idea does indeed constitute our very nature, then this must, of necessity, also be our *possibility*: the possibility that lets us be the human beings that we are. If the Devil, by contrast, was the unthinkable (and thus the tempting) impossibility of God, human beings are themselves the possibility of God: *His opportunity* to be, to exist at all. What is more, a *unique* opportunity, just as the Son of Man who is the Son of God is unique. In their life, suffering, and death, it is human beings who open the ways of the Lord. For it is only in human beings that re-flection, that *return*, can transpire. The sacrifice of man *makes a place* for God, shows and reveals Him as the Lack, that is to say, as *pro-mise*. As such He is unreachable. The feeling of that inaccessibility is suffering and, at the most extreme, death. The knowledge of this feeling, the knowledge of the imminence of death, is "the awakening of consciousness within man himself, and this is the history which is repeated in very human being."[8] By virtue of this feeling we are finite and mortal, while by virtue of this knowing we are infinite. But this latter is, of course, the infinitude *of* mortality. To know that we are dying: this is *the word of God*. For "when we say the infinite is the *not*-finite, we have thereby indeed already uttered the truth, for since the finite is the first negative, the not-finite is the negation of the negation, that is, the negation that is identical with itself and thus at the same time true affirmation" (*Enz.* §94, *Zusatz*; *W.* 8, 200; Dahlstrom I, 150).

This is our debt and our transgression; this is our mission. The liminal opposition of the finite and the infinite becomes the "return" from this scission, preserving and maintaining that fissure as an internal moment of reconciliation: "the standpoint of division is likewise to be sublated [*aufzuheben*], and spirit is to return to oneness by its own means [*durch sich*]" (*Enz.* §24, *Zusatz* 3; *W.* 8, 88); Dahlstrom I, 64). Through itself and by means of itself: not through human beings *alone*, as if "man" could be an expression with any meaning if he were indeed abandoned by the hand of God. Spirit is the self-consciousness of God in man's own consciousness of infinite subjectivity. If it is true that man is "the temple of God and that the Spirit of God dwells" there,[9] it is no less true that there is no content without the one who receives it, but also, and above all, that only when the receiver has been *emptied* and *broken* can the content give itself to be seen.

2. Man as the Possibility of God: *Passio Christi*

A double movement takes place here: *first*, the consciousness of being the place, the possibility of God, raises man above his natural particularity, in which he was engulfed and through which he remained enslaved. Raised in this way to the level of totality, he ceases to be *one of a number of others*, an exclusion that repels the many from itself: he ceases to be an expression of *evil*. The human being, having thus become by contrast an example in each unique case, has to accomplish the *passio Christi* within himself: *Einmal ist Allemal*. Once is always. Yet not because this one time—the death of the Redeemer—would be sufficient, and we might thereby find ourselves liberated from suffering and death (thus taking on, in short, *the part of the Devil*). Nor again because, if this is to transpire always or at "all times," it would always be exactly the same, thus diluting its unique and exemplary significance. This Hegelian proposition is, of course, a *speculative* proposition: only if "all times," taken one by one, is this *unique* or one and only time: only if we die in Christ and die with Christ does Redemption possess any meaning. It is the Redemption from the presumption of innocence, from the absence of culpability. All human beings are culpable as long as they fail, through self-sacrifice, to prove otherwise: as long as they fail to expiate their transgressions. The Apostle tells us: "Christ is risen from the dead as the first of those that die." In the Lutheran Bible used by Hegel, we read: "Christ is risen from the dead and has become the first [*der Erstling*] of those that sleep."[10] Christ as the Prince of the dead? The Resurrection would thus be a way of preserving-and-maintaining-oneself (*sich erhalten*) through *the knowing of oneself as dead*. And this is, in effect, the *second* element of the movement: Christ does not descend, *as* Christ, on the community of the faithful. He is dead, and remains dead. It is the *Paraklētos* that descends (the *Paraclete*, from the verb *parakaleo*: to call or send for help). Not the man Jesus, the man born out of wedlock, the man without a country, who happened to be born in Judea, and who grew up in Galilee, the man without a Kingdom in this world. For now, all particularity has been left behind. It is not a man who descends, but fire and flame (at once illuminating and destructive); it speaks no language (let alone Aramaic), but it bestows the gift of tongues. It is the Spirit "that bloweth where it listeth." With the coming of the Spirit all and every "Beyond" has been dispelled. And for a start, the beyond of the abstraction of the Father, of that inert and painless immanence from which God himself flees as from his own diabolical ground. But the empirical givenness of the Son is also cancelled: the beyond of the *flesh*, of Nature as the falling-away of the Idea. Universality and particularity are henceforth taken up in the *concrete singularity* of the Spirit. This is neither *logos* nor *phusis*, but event: the happening of History.

In place of the fate or destiny of the ancients, of inflexible and unyielding *heimarmēnē*, there rises the Paraclete, the Comforter. And in this sense we can say that "the Christian religion is to be regarded as the religion of consolation and, indeed, of absolute consolation" (*Enz.* §147, *Zusatz* (*W.* 8, 291); Dahlstrom I, 220). Yet in the eyes of Hegel, we would simply turn Christianity into a demonic religion (if it is indeed certain that *Eigensinn*, or love of self, is the nature of Evil), if by "consolation" here we were to understand the promise of a better life, as a kind of *Ersatz* or compensatory substitute for present sufferings. For the idea of consolation actually "acquires a completely different and higher meaning." The help that is offered lies rather in teaching us how to bear our own cross: to avoid casting on others (on the Other, or on that alterity that is Nature) the responsibility for what happens to us: "each of us forges his own fate." Here is where true freedom is to be encountered: we ask forgiveness of one another (and Spirit is this supreme mutuality) for our own transgressions in recognizing that "what happens to man is only an evolution of himself and that he bears only his own guilt, and thereby comports himself as a free being" (*W.* 8, 292; Dahlstrom I, 221). But we have already seen that what we bear as our own substantial nature is the divine Idea. *It is this Idea which is our own guilt.* Culpable for not being God, just as the eternal Father himself—without the supreme sacrifice of his Son—would be culpable for not being Man. Reconciliation, redemption, transpires on both sides here: the unity of divine and human nature holds "not only for the definition of human nature but just as much for the DIVINE NATURE" (*V-Rel.* 5, 46; Hodgson 3, 110).

Let us consider this convergence of contrary directions in more concrete detail. In the first place, there is no simply private religion, religion that pertains solely to the individual. "True religion and true religiosity springs solely from ethical life, and is a thinking ethical life, namely one which has become aware of the free universality of its concrete essence" (*Enz.* §552, *Anm.* (*W.* 10, 394f.); Wallace, 283). In this sense, therefore, to *think* one's own ethical life (family, civil society, people, political state) is precisely to live in a religious way for Hegel. It is not a question of dreaming of other far-away worlds, but rather of making this world of human beings a livable and habitable one (for that is what the word "ethical" properly signifies). In this sense we can say that religion is the result of society, insofar as the latter, if it is to sustain itself, needs to reflect on the processes that constitute it. And such reflection is what *opens up to freedom*, if freedom is indeed *self-determination*, the infinite mediation of my particular determinateness (everything that conditions and pro-duces me) and of my abstract singularity (the "I" of my arbitrary will) (*Enz.* §480 (*W.* 10, 300); Wallace, 238). *To be free is to take over what happens to me*, to convert my determinateness into determination, and to make this into the *basis* of my personality. Thus the one who is free is not one who, like a merely *natural* being, passively accepts gender, work, and power as a given. Nor are those free who attempt, in the name of a world wholly beyond this one, to escape from this *lacrimorum valle*, and abstractly elect to negate the world of the family (through vows of chastity), that of civil society (through vows of poverty), or that of the political state (through vows of obedience either to some "unwritten law" or some law that is presumed to be higher than the laws of man). This kind of (ultimately parasitic) withdrawal from the world, which is typical of the Catholic religion according to Hegel, finds itself confronted instead with the institutions of ethical life: marriage and family life, activity in the legitimate acquisition of material goods and probity in the exchange and management of capital, obedience to the law and the demand and perspectives of the political state. The world thus finds itself effectively de-sacralized in the name of ethical life: "what in the world was meant to be *holiness* [*Heiligkeit*] is supplanted [*verdrängt*] by ethical life" (*W.* 10, 356; Wallace, 286). Long before the Weber's thematization of these questions, we find that Hegel, the thinker of the bourgeois world, has already moved toward a radical disenchantment of the world (*Entzauberung der Welt*).

Yet it would also be a one-sided, and thus mistaken, approach to emphasize this movement alone and contend (enthusiastically or despondently, according to one's ideological outlook) that Hegel has thus simply turned religion into a useless trace or echo, an inheritance from the dark ages that is now to be cast aside, and simply chosen to celebrate the ineluctable course of modernizing secularization. The result of every dialectical process, as we all know, is in truth the *grounding* of the elements that have come to produce it. There is nothing is more alien to Hegel than attempting to transform process into *genesis* in some kind of linear manner. Ethical life is doing nothing but exposing, in a reflexive and *essential* way, that which effectively constitutes it. There would be no objective spirit without absolute spirit, just as there has been no true society (which is more than a collection of "reasonable and egoistic" atoms) without religion: "for self-consciousness religion is the basis of ethical life and the state" (*W.* 10, 356; Wallace, 284). It is not that Hegel divinizes society as such (that would be a genuine catastrophe, and we should not forget that it is Carl Schmitt who specifically talks about *Politische Theologie*), or tries to turn God into society (the State is our ethical *substance* (*Enz.* §535; *W.* 10, 330; Wallace, 263–64), but it is not the *concept* of the ethical). The sacred has not so much disappeared as it has been significantly displaced. It no longer lies in Nature (as it did in what Hegel calls the "determinate religions"), nor does it lie in society (as in Calvinism, at least according to Hegel's—partly incorrect—conception of it, a question to which we shall return in what follows). It lies rather in the *community* (*Gemeinde*) of free human beings, a community that—we should hasten to add—is certainly not some sort of caste or hierarchy set apart from society. For this community is essentially a higher way of regarding society: not on the basis of economic relations or the structures of political administration, but in terms of the *symbolic* role of this community in generating a meaningful account that can further truth and the continuing significance of the family, civil society, and the state. A genuine divine history, namely one that has been fully grasped conceptually, relegates the sensible history of Christ the man to the domain of what is sensibly past and gone.[11]

Thus, the community of which Hegel speaks is not a Church, if Hegel is right in claiming (and twisting *pro domo sua* the reality of the different Lutheran confessions) that: "With *Protestants, priests* are only *teachers* (*Lehrer*). All in the community are equal before God as the present Spirit of the community."[12] In short, the religious community, as Hegel conceives it, is the *absolute truth* of the State: namely that which gives meaning, value, and stability to the latter. That is why Hegel sees it as "the monstrous error of our times" to claim that we can separate church and state or treat them as externally related and simply external to one another (*Enz.* §552, *Anm.*; *W.* 10, 356; Wallace, 284). This inseparability does not, of course, imply submission on the part of the State to any determinate Church, as in a *theocracy* (that would be an equally tremendous error in turn), nor a transformation of a Church into the ideological appendage of the State (which is Hegel's view of Anglicanism). State and religion have the same referent for Hegel: *a union of free self-conscious human beings in the context of a historical people.* Thus, religion is the reflexion, or rather the subjective unfolding or development (*Entwicklung* as understood in accordance with the *logic of the Concept*), of the ethical substance that constitutes the state. And for this reason the activity of the community has to be the same as that of the society within the state, but an activity that lends a symbolic value of recognition and cohesion to the *Gemeinde*. Or, precisely, lends to its actions the significance of a *sacrament*. Marriage, work, and obedience to the law have what Hegel calls "the cultus" as both their result and their foundation: the union of the word (*logos*) and of work or labor (*phusis* in reflected form) in the context of free self-consciousness, something that thereby *sacralizes* the ethical institutions. This signifies, no less, not only that society possesses meaning solely in the cultus of the community, but also (as the co-inciding movement of divine descent) that God, fully grasped as spirit, exists *only* in this cultus. For the latter is nothing other than the eternal process through which "the subject knows the absolute substance into which it has to sublate itself to be at the same time its essence, its substance, in which, therefore, self-consciousness is implicitly conserved" (*V-Rel.* 3, 97; Hodgson I, 189).

3. Cultus and Eucharist as *Manducatio Spiritualis*

On this understanding of it, the cultus is *the highest shape* of the development of spirit as expounded in the *Encyclopaedia*, which begins with "abstract being," in that conceptual determinacy and the realm of "representation" are unified in the context of the cultus (*V-Rel.* 3, 58; Hodgson 1, 144–45). In other words, this is the place where representation is fully assumed as the Concept and where the subject internalizes and re-collects itself as (the knowing of) essential being. It is here, in the cultus, that the encyclopedic and the phenomenological exposition come harmoniously together, for this is the very point where phenomenological "appearing" (*Erscheinung*: the matter of the sacraments) becomes equal to the essence (*Wesen*: the divine substance that has been interiorized), and where, therefore, the exposition or presentation (*Darstellung*: the ceremony of the cultus) "coincides with the authentic Science of spirit" (*Phä. GW* 9: 622–25; Miller, 57). Here, in other words, man knows himself in God and God knows himself in man.

Now in spite of its function as the supreme form of reconciliation, this ceremony does not cease to be *symbolic* in character insofar as it still presents a certain *irrecuperable* dimension (emphatically for example in the physical destruction of what is consumed in the Eucharist or the destruction of the body in the Rite of Extreme Unction). The cultus continues to remain a *shape* of spirit that is still to be *reflexively* appropriated in thought. This truth of the cultus is philosophical knowing itself. And that is why we can say that "philosophy is theology, and our occupation with it—or rather in it—is of itself the service of God" (*Gottesdienst*; see *V-Rel.* 3, 4; Hodgson 1, 84). Here it should be clearly understood that philosophy does not compete with religion by elaborating a distinct cultus of its own that would somehow be higher than religion itself. Rather, what philosophy adds to the religious cultus is *the knowledge of the insuperable imperfection of the latter*, a mark in turn of the ineliminable difference between God and man, the infinite and the finite, a difference that is *accomplished* in the abnegation and sacrifice of the latter in favor of the former, something that is only *represented* in a ceremonial and vicarious way: the Bread and Wine as if they were the Body and Blood of Christ or, definitively, the life of each and every human being.

Without this representational dimension it would be impossible to supply the required sustenance, the *Rückkehr zum Leben*, that provides validity and lends solidity and permanence to the objective ethical institutions. Yet that same dimension requires the self-suppression or *suicide* of the natural aspect[13] to open the way for the Phoenix of Absolute Spirit. And, in effect, this destruction is realized: this is what happens in the *manducatio* of the Eucharist in its most radical, namely Lutheran, form. But this destructions is only accomplished momentarily on each occasion of the cultus, and for that reason remains subjected, in phenomenological terms, to the dialectic of the *Jetztpunkt*, the Now, and logically to the dialectic of *Werden*, of the process of becoming.

For all of its tremendous majesty, then, the cultus (and the community that is bound up with it) sees itself overtaken or superseded by this temporal becoming. The difference, abolished on each particular occasion, nonetheless sees itself restored, or fixed, *in a point* (this is the infinite sadness that "the Now" passes into the solidity of the *es war*, of the "it was"). And this sensible character of the ceremony of the cultus turns the real and present reconciliation into a historical event (*ein historisches Ereignis*). The real presence of Spirit in the sacrament is *punctual* in character, and *passes away*; and with this the community also passes away, incapable of recognizing the actuality that has *always already been accomplished*, although only *für uns*, for us, namely the *community of philosophy*.

At the end of the path that is traced in the *Encyclopaedia* (a path that is more of a *circuit, ein Ring*), then, the religious community has not relinquished the realm of *yearning* finitude, of that melancholia that was magisterially described by the Stagirite. The mode of life that belongs to the Aristotelian God lies in the uninterrupted exercise of that which "is given only briefly to us human beings to enjoy" (*Metaphysics*, XII, 1072b, 15f.). Wakefulness, sensation, intellection are what is most agreeable, in effect, since to wake is to *be* awake, to sense and feel is to *be* sensing and feeling, to see is to *be* seeing: the present expands, broadens its reach, encompasses within itself the past that it produces. Yet that present is a *lapse*: it runs and passes. If we wish to fix or arrest it, we ourselves have to *run through* the process of hopes and memories; yet these possess a sort of bloodless or borrowed life. They cling to the *phantasma* of what is still to come or of what has been.

But after all that we have just said, it is permissible to ask ourselves if the Hegelian conception of things may not be infinitely more tragic than the Aristotelian one precisely because God not only takes a certain pleasure in blood, but himself flows and bleeds away in the act of human sacrifice, and only eternally recovers himself in the *knowing* of the evanescent character of that sacrifice: in the knowing of the ineluctable pastness or *Vergangenheit* of the community. If it is true—to introduce Aristotle once again—that the truth pure and simple gives itself in a *thigein kai phanai*,[14] then that which affects *itself* and lets *itself* shine forth in all speech (for Spirit is this "itself" that is at once impersonal and reflexive) is *the presentness of the past*: the conjunction involved here is co-agency, is *contingency*. The truth does not offer the reason that accounts for error, but is itself the *reason for erring*. The supreme blessing is the supreme curse: *summum ius summa inuria*. In the cultus God lives the death of mortals. *He is this death*.

Hence I believe that we should not be so surprised by the ultimate re-course of Hegel's thought: when in effect his thought arrives at the ultimate shape or figure, the Community and the Cultus, it does not deploy for its *Deduktion* the final and most fully developed of the logical determinations (the doctrine of the Absolute Idea, let us say), but the first, the poorest, and the most abstract development, namely the *logic of becoming*: *Entstehen, Bestehen, Vergehen*, "a birth, a conservation, a passing away" of the community.[15] The *Mitte* or middle term here ("the being of the community") is the cultus—a *broken* middle term that suffers dispersal through the dialectic of the "now."

The community is born in and through faith, it is conserved in the cultus, and it passes away or perishes *continually* (in the dialectic of continuity and discreteness that is proper—once again—to the logic of being) in that it conflates the eternal reconciliation with a sensible representation (and in the sense of a ritual "ceremony" as well). That is why the content of the truth of religion inevitably seeks refuge in the Concept (*in den Begriff flüchtet*).[16] Thus we are unable, now, to avoid the highly disconcerting conclusion that a *universal* reconciliation in its own right is then impossible (it would be futile and even counterproductive to try and realize such reconciliation in the realm of praxis and history, as the Young Hegelians expressly wanted to do, since history itself is a *Schädelstätte*, a Golgotha, a demonstration of the futility, *within time*, of all efforts to attain such reconciliation. Thus just as to be free, on the individual level, is to assume one's own guilt and responsibility, so too on the collective and universal level to enjoy reconciliation is precisely to acknowledge in thought the irreconcilability of Nature and Spirit, once again and for always to acknowledge the *errance of reason*. For religion alone is "the mode of consciousness in which the truth exists for all human beings, exists for all human beings whatever their level of culture and education [*Bildung*]. The philosophical knowledge [*wissenschaftliches Erkennen*] of truth, however, is a particular mode of consciousness of the truth, the labor of which not all, indeed only a few, undertake."[17] Thus the *Gemeinde der Philosophie*, the only community that could properly accede to the Truth, comes to constitute, paradoxically enough, an "isolated order of priests—a sanctuary" (*Priesterstand isoliert—Heiligtum*). And reconciliation, redemption, continues to remain, for always, something "partial" (*partiell*) (See *V-Rel.* 5, 97; Hodgson 3, 162).

4. The Spirit as the Wound of Time

Let us look more closely at this intimate or inner tragedy of philosophy, this wound of Spirit that Spirit cannot close because *Spirit itself is the wound of time*. Precisely there where the community ought to be able to conserve itself and attain its authentic being, preserved between the terrible extremes of *generatio* and *corruptio*, that is to say, precisely in the *cultus*, is the very place where the Christian community breaks apart and disintegrates into opposing sects (*V-Rel.* 5, 88; Hodgson 3, 154). It is in regard to the highest ritual representation of all, namely the Eucharist (*Abendmahl*), that Catholicism, Lutheranism, and Calvinism clearly reveal their irreconcilable differences, which all have to do with the appropriate *spiritual* relation to nature, to time, and to memory. The desired *unio mystica* is supposed to be, at one and the same time, the conservation of the community *in* the constant (re)creation and conservation of the world *by means of* the "eternal *repetition* of the life, passion, and resurrection of Christ in the *members* of the church" (*V-Rel.* 5, 88; Hodgson 3, 152). However, the Catholic conception fixes and isolates the material and *natural* aspect of the Eucharist precisely because it admits the real presence of God in the *host*, even when the latter is not actually consumed. For the Lutheran conception, by contrast, the host possesses significance solely in terms of faith and the *communio* itself: it is only the physical destruction and consumption of the bread and wine, simultaneously accompanied by the sacred words and the subjective act of acknowledgment and interiorization, that allows, *in the very act* of sacred *manducatio*, the presence of Spirit to arise. Yet this act is *eo ipso* a moment that passes, an evanescent quantity. God gives himself only in this *transition* itself. But lacking precisely this *mystical* element, Calvinism ultimately transforms this sacred presence simply into "a memorial, an ordinary psychological relationship; everything speculative [has] disappeared, being absorbed in the relationship of the community."[18] Here indeed, in Calvinism, we can see a completed form of secularization, and Hegel will himself endorse, *avant la lettre*, the Weberian thesis of the *Entzauberung der Welt*. For all this, it is not without significance that both in his autograph manuscript and his subsequent series of lectures it is this psychologically oriented Calvinist reading that occupies the final place, whereas Lutheranism remains located in the middle. This sits rather well (although it presents certain problems with regard to Hegel's personal position as a self-confessed Lutheran) with the philosophico-historical consideration that the process of Enlightenment and the triumph of the calculative "understanding" over speculative reason (even if the latter may take flight—and it is indeed significant that we should talk of "refuge" here—to philosophy) has produced an incurable discord (*Misston*: *V-Rel.* 5, 94; Hodgson 3, 158).

It is in effect incurable, at least in the present state of the world. And the conclusion of Hegel's lecture manuscript of 1821 must in effect appear scandalous and almost inconceivable for those who accept the standard image of an optimistic and complacent Hegel: "Unconcerned about how it may go with the world; [philosophy] cannot become involved with it [*mit ihr nicht zusammengehen*] [. . .] How things *take shape* [in the world] is not *our affair*" (*V-Rel*. 5, 97; Hodgson 3, 162).

But if philosophy cannot become involved with the way of the world, is this not itself proof of its failure? Was the ultimate meaning and purpose of this science not supposed to be "the reconciliation of self-conscious reason with the reason that is—in other words, with actuality"? (*Enz.* §6; *W.* 8, 47; Dahlstrom I, 33). It was indeed. And it is precisely for this reason that philosophy cannot, *in principle*, become involved with the world, although it must certainly be concerned *with the truth of the world*. And this truth is that its "existence [*Dasein*] in general is partly appearance [*Erscheinung*] and only partly actuality" (*Enz.* §6; *W.* 8, 48; Dahlstrom I, 33). Nor can philosophy presume, without falling into mere edification or prophetic posturing (that is, without ceasing to be *the thinking consideration of things*), to take on the role of instructing the world as to how it *ought* to be, although it is not yet so, or indeed not so at all. What philosophy grasps is the very *failure* of the world to raise itself to the Idea. In the extreme case: the failure of the religious and the political community to raise itself to Absolute Spirit, apart from certain privileged instants (in the activity of the cultus) that must be incessantly renewed and that thus also constantly run the risk of turning into merely empty ceremonies, falling into a representation and performance of the theater of memory. Philosophy is the thinking that thinks that risk, and that thinks that fall. In the best possible case we can say that it thinks the feelings of the *heart* and a representation of the *intellect*, while both remain divorced from one another, torn apart in the scandalous predicament of a people that relies on the simple and immediate faith of the heart—one that appeals to the sensuous and thus falls into a fanaticism of the imagination and the idolatry of a divinized nature—and of an *enlightened* stratum of society that converts the life of spirit into a theatrical simulacrum: an enlightenment that turns into *dis-enlightenment*, a clearing up into a clearing out (*Ausklärung*) (*V-Rel*. 5, 96; Hodgson 3, 160).

The Errancy of Reason (The Perishing of the Community)   131

Christ spoke to his disciples, saying: "Ye are the salt of the earth: but if the salt have lost his savor, wherewith shall it be salted?" (in Luther's version: "Wo nun das Salz *dumm* wird [. . .]"—literally: if the salt is become *dull or insipid*).[19] Is this a kind of warning or a premonition, an anticipation of what would necessarily come to pass? Hegel seems to have believed the latter. The Christian community (which appears to have been won over for the cause of Calvinism, although in an external and theatrical fashion it still claims to be faithful to Catholicism or Lutheranism) has abandoned the infinite anguish that is equally a manifestation of infinite love in favor of "enjoyment, and a love without anguish." Now, "when the Gospel is preached in a *naturalistic way*—there *the salt has lost its savor*" (*V-Rel.* 5, 95; Hodgson 3, 160).

Are we faced with an emphatically *empirical* consideration here, even on the part of Hegel—something more common than one might think—a consideration that simply and accurately records what reality offers him, even if this ruptures the all-encompassing structure of the system itself? Or faced rather with a *metaphysical* conception (and an ultimately nihilistic one) in the sense that things have always been so and will always be so, while philosophy, *au dessous de la mêlée*, and impotent though it is, administers advice from on high about what in truth *ought* to be? Such a disjunction, of course, is completely inadequate here. The entirety of Hegel's thought was dedicated from the first to challenging this kind of fixed division between facts and theory, along with the corresponding conception of truth as "adequation" or correctness. Speculative thinking as Hegel understands it consists precisely in the dissolution of a hiatus such as this. There is no "time" on the one hand confronted by some empty "eternity" on the other. "But when the fullness of the time was come, God sent forth his Son, made of a woman, made under the law."[20] The time is ready, the time is fulfilled, when nature (the mother) and *logos* (the law) reveal their unilateral character and enter into their own result-and-ground: when spirit, recollecting and interiorizing itself, knows its infinitude and substantiality in the subject of immediate self-consciousness, in infinite negativity (*V-Rel.* 5, 80; Hodgson 3, 144). What can negate this subject, other than the abstraction of its emergence? Spirit is pure relation and, therefore, the liquefaction of the extremes. It knows that "the Logical" manifests itself in the world, though precisely as the *very* negativity of the latter. It does not condemn the world: it is the world that condemns itself in opening itself to the *Verbum Dei*. Yet this condemnation is the glory of God. There is no other. God appears in the flesh, as a sensible presence. He thereby opens history. But that history, being immediate, has passed. And when one attempts to explicate the historical event (*Geschichte*) solely by reference to the historiographical (*Historie*), to the dead weight of the "so it was," then everything is finished: *so ist es aus*.[21] Yet that everything is finished, that time has devoured itself, is something *necessary*. Here too the times have been fulfilled, for "the time has come [*erfüllet ist*] when the need [*Bedürfnis*] lies in justification through the concept—[the truth] is no longer justified in terms of faith" (*V-Rel.* 5, 95; Hodgson, 159–60). Yet (*pace* Luther) there has *never* been justification by faith for Hegel. The time that is fulfilled through the coming of the Son and the time that is fulfilled through seeking *refuge* in the Concept is *one and the same time*: the one and only time of history, *the time that is exhausted*, that can no longer yield anything more. The necessity of comprehending what has come to pass is itself inscribed in the passion and death of Christ. *Consummatum est: es ist aus*. It is only at the margin of the world that the philosopher can comprehend that the death of Christ necessarily, logically, involved the perishing of the community. It is only the isolated position of philosophy that can sustain the infinite anguish of the finitude of man, of the mortality of man. The consciousness of mortality is itself immortality, is itself eternity. For it is the pure knowing that everything must perish in order that the Whole should be preserved. *Changing, it rests.*

Yet this marginality is not a demonic one. Contemplation is the *theoria* of our own irreparable ephemerality. Philosophy does not say: this is how human beings should think and act, let us say, in the religious and political domain; it offers no instant recipe, no "care of the soul," it does not tell us which particular saving doctrines or further resources for the contrite soul are requisite if we would escape the destructive threats that shadow this domain. On the contrary, philosophy shows the inner coherence, the significant interconnection, that shapes and informs how the human beings

The Errancy of Reason (The Perishing of the Community)   133

at the end of Modernity, at the end of Christianity, act and think. There is no alternative here. The reconciliation is a reconciliation with grief and with death and, for this reason, with the infinite love of Death for the sake of the dead.

5. The Fullness of Time as the Exhaustion of Time

The young Hegel, of the years between 1800 and 1804, perhaps influenced by a certain Gnosticism (I am not sure if Hegel has ever read Joachim of Fiore), had dreamt of a third and ultimate form of religion that would arise from the exhausted body of Christianity.[22] Beyond the Catholic sacralization (i.e., the superstitious veneration) of empirical existence, beyond the Protestantism that dried up the sacred in the name of ethical endeavor so that "life has become a common unhallowed workaday matter (*Werktag*),"[23] there would have to emerge a new religion "when there is a *free people* and Reason has found once more its reality as an ethical spirit."[24] Hegel never abandoned this ideal of such a union between freedom, reason, and ethical life. What he abandoned was only the *mystical belief* that this union would have to involve something resembling an apocalyptic Second Coming: namely the end of times. In fact, this union has *already* come to pass [. . .] *in* the world (if not here, then where?). This is because freedom involves the assumption of one's own responsibility, reason the burden of errance and contingency, and authentic ethical life the mutual forgiveness of sins. If this is so, then we already stand—since time has been fulfilled—in that *pax Dei* that, contrary to the Apostle, is not higher than all reason precisely because it is reason itself.[25] This is the peace that constantly reveals itself as *universal history*, precisely as that slaughterhouse that Hegel speaks of when he refers to the "sadness" that "oppresses us to think that the finest manifestations of life must perish in history, and that we walk among the ruins of excellence." Everything for which we feel a living interest is torn away from us by history. "The passions have spelt its ruin; for it is all transient" (*es ist vergänglich*).[26]

This peace amid the ruins, is it the peace of God? Yet it is only amid the ruins that new life springs forth. This is hardly the Second

Coming, nor indeed a Third Religion. Here too, *Einmal ist Allemal*. We have always lived amid the ruins, and lived from these ruins. And we too, animals that we are, *der Kampf selbst*, the struggle itself, in our innermost being, are a ruin of ruins. The philosopher beholds, in serenity, the crumbling away of all that is. The philosopher knows that knowing is also opaque to itself. He knows that if religion seeks refuge in the Concept, it is he—like the Flaming Angel—whose Concept guards the life that ceaselessly passes into death, a death that is recalled and interiorized in life. This is the double movement that silently guards our thoughts: these *sterbliche Gedanken*.

One must, in all truth, be Hegel to bear so much blood.

Notes

Notes to Foreword

1. *Metaphysics*, I. 2, 982a4: *tēn epistēmēn zētoumen*. (Henceforth cited directly in the text).
2. *Kritik der reinen Vernunft*, A 737/B 765 edited by R. Schmidt, Hamburg, 1956 (*Critique of Pure Reason*, translated by Norman Kemp Smith, London, 1933).

Notes to Chapter I

1. C. Alexandre, *Dictionnaire Grec-Français*, Paris 1878, 1492 (the entry under *hypokeimai*). The entry in the standard *Greek-English Lexicon* by H. G. Liddell and Robert Scott, Oxford 1968, 1884, includes the following elucidations of this verb: "1. to be established, set before one (by oneself or another) as an aim or principle [. . .] 2. to be assumed as a hypothesis [. . .] 3. To be suggested [. . .] 4. to be in prospect [. . .] 5. to be subject to, submit to [. . .] 6. to be subject to, liable to a penalty [. . .] 7. to be pledged [. . .] 8. to underlie, as the foundation in which something else inheres, to be implied or presupposed by something else [. . .] to exist [. . .] to be subject or subordinate [. . .] 9. to be the subject-matter"; while the Supplement adds (145): "to be put before the audience in the theatre." The abridged version of the Lexicon (Oxford 1991) cites the following meanings: "to lie under or below [. . .] to be put under the eyes, to be set or proposed before one [. . .] to be laid down, assumed, taken for granted [. . .] to be suggested [. . .] to be left at bottom, left remaining, reserved [. . .] to be subject to, submit [. . .] to form the subject or matter."
2. Aristotle (*Metaphysics* I. 2, 983a, 27–29): "We call one cause the substance (*tēn ousian*) or the 'what it is to be,' or strictly the 'what it was

to be' (*to ti ēn einai*), of the thing (since the 'reason why' of a thing is ultimately reducible to its formula (*ton logon*) and the ultimate 'reason why' is a cause and principle." (We should note the *reflexive* circularity that is expressed here: to say what something *in the last instance* really is, its ultimate *logos*, amounts to affirming all the affections, properties, and determinations of that thing).

3. *Ethica Ordine Geometrico demonstrata*. Pars V. Pr. XXIII, Scholium.

4. *Differenz des Fichteschen und Schellingschen Systems der Philosophie. W.* 2, 36–37 (*The Difference between Fichte's and Schelling's System of Philosophy*, translated by H. S. Harris and Walter Cerf, New York, NY 1977, 105).

5. *De anima*, Bk. III, 8, 431b, 21–22: "hē psychē ta onta pōs esti panta."

6. *Wissenschaft der Logik* (= *WdL*). *Die objektive Logik*. 2. Buch (1. Abschn., 2. Kap., C.3, Anm. 3). *Gesammelte Werke* (= *GW*), Hamburg 1978; 11: 290: "Im gewöhnlichen Schliessen erscheint das *Seyn* des Endlichen als Grund des Absoluten; darum weil Endliches *ist*, ist das Absolute. Die Wahrheit aber ist, daß darum, weil das Endliche der an sich selbst widersprechende Gegensatz, weil es *nicht ist*, das Absolute ist. In jenem Sinne lautet der Satz des Schlusses so: 'Das *Seyn* des Endlichen ist das *Seyn* des Absoluten'; in diesem Sinne aber so: 'Das *Nichtseyn* des Endlichen ist das *Seyn* des Absoluten.'" ("In customary inference, the *being* of the *being* of the finite appears to be the ground of the absolute; because the finite *is*, the absolute is. But the truth is that the absolute is because the finite is the immanently self-contadictory opposition, because it *is not*. In the former meaning, the conclusion is that 'the *being* of the finite is the being of the absolute'; but in the latter, that 'the non-being of the finite is the *being* of the absolute.'").

7. *Faust I. Studierzimmer*, vv. 1936–39, Stuttgart 1971, 56. See *Faust*, translated by Walter Arndt, New York, NY 1976, 51: "Who would know and describe a living thing, / Seeks first to expel the spirit within, / Then he stands there, the parts held in his grasp, / Lost just the spiritual bond, alas!"

8. *Phänomenologie des Geistes*, Hamburg 1980. *GW* 9, 18; Hegel's peculiar form of expression here has presented a problem for translation: A.V. Miller renders the phrase as follows: "[. . .] everything turns on grasping and expressing the True, not only as *Substance*, but equally as *Subject*" (*Hegel's Phenomenology of Spirit*, Oxford 1970, 10); J. B. Baillie, on the other hand, writes: "[. . .] everything depends on grasping and expressing the ultimate truth not as Substance but as Subject as well" (*The Phenomenology of Mind*, first published 1910, reprinted New York, NY 1967, 80), and Yirmiyahu Yovel translates similarly: "[. . .] everything depends on comprehending and expressing the true not as substance, but equally also as subject" (*Hegel's Preface to the "Phenomenology of Spirit,"* Princeton, NJ 2005, 95).

9. See *Enz.* (1830) (= *Enz.*) §20, *Anm.*; *W.* 8, 74: "Was ich nur *meine*, ist *mein*, gehört mir als diesem besonderen Individuum an; wenn aber dies Sprache nur Allgemeines ausdrückt, so kann ich nicht sagen, was ich nur *meine*"; see *Encyclopedia of the Philosophical Sciences in Basic Outline*, translated by Klaus Brinkmann and Daniel O. Dahlstrom, Cambridge, 2010, 52: "What I only *mean*, is *mine*, belonging to me as this particular individual. If, however, language expresses only what is universal, then I cannot say what I *mean* only." See also Hegel's *Vorlesungen über die Geschichte der Philosophie* (edited by Michelet / Irrlitz-Gurst, Berlin 1984, 20), *Einleitung* A. 1.1 a: "Eine Meinung ist eine subjective Vorstellung, ein beliebiger Gedanke, eine Einbildung, die ich so oder so und ein anderer anders haben kann; eine Meinung ist mein, sie ist nicht ein in sich allgemeiner, an und für sich seiender Gedanke." (From the Introduction to Hegel's *Lectures on the History of Philosophy*: "An opinion is a subjective representation, an arbitrary thought, a conceit or passing fancy that I may entertain in some way or other, and which others may entertain quite differently; my opinion is mine, it is not an intrinsically universal thought which holds in and for itself.")

10. English translations of Hegel sometimes exploit the similarity between "concept" and "comprehension" to bring out the connection between *Begriff* and *begreifen*, between "grasping" something and "gathering" the moments of a concrete whole in a single perspective.

11. See *Enz.* §238, Zusatz; *W.* 8, 390f.: "das philosophische Denken [. . .] erweist sich als die Tätigkeit des Begriffs selbst. Dazu aber gehört die Anstrengung, die eigenen Einfälle und besonderen Meinungen, welche sich immer hervortun wollen, von sich abzuhalten." (tr. p. 301).

12. *Enz.* §21, Zusatz; *W.* 8, 77; tr. 55.
13. *Enz.* §21, *W.* 8, 76; tr. 54.
14. *Enz.* §23, *W.* 8, 80; tr. 57.
15. *Enz.* §24, *W.* 8, 80f.; tr. 58.
16. *Enz.* §22, *W.* 8, 78; tr. 56.
17. *Enz.* §24, *W.* 8, 81; tr. 58.

18. *WdL. GW 2. Buch* (2. Abschn., 2. Kap., A.); *GW* 11, 344: "Das Gesetz ist also das Positive der Vermittlung des Erscheinenden. Die Erscheinung ist zunächst die Existenz als die *negative* Vermittlung mit sich, so daß das Existierende durch sein *eigenes Nichtbestehen*, durch ein Anderes, und wieder durch das *Nichtbestehen dieses Anderen* mit sich vermittelt ist. Darin ist enthalten *erstens* das bloße Scheinen und das Verschwinden beider, die unwesentliche Erscheinung, *zweitens* auch das *Bleiben* oder das *Gesetz*; denn *jedes* der beiden *existiert* in jenem Aufheben des Anderen, und ihr Gesetztsein als ihre Negativität ist zugleich das *identische*, *positive* Gesetztsein beider." ("The law is therefore the positive side of the mediation of

what appears. Appearance is at first Existence as negative self-mediation, so that the existent is mediated with itself through its *own non-subsistence*, through an other, and, again, through the *non-subsistence of this other*. In this is contained *first*, the mere illusory being and the vanishing of both, the unessential Appearance, *secondly*, also their *permanence* or *law*, for *each* of the two *exists* in the sublating of the other, and their positedness as their negativity is at the same time the *identical, positive* positedness of both.")

19. Vergil, *Aeneid*. VI, vv. 126–29: "the downward path to the underworld / Is easy; all the livelong night and day / Dark Pluto's door stands open for a guest. / But O! remounting to the world of light, / This is a task indeed, a strife supreme."

20. *WdL. Die subjektive Logik* (3. Abschn., 3. *Kap.*); *GW* 12: 236: "Die absolute Idee als der vernünftige Begriff, der in seiner Realität nur mit sich selbst zusammengeht, ist um dieser Unmittelbarkeit seiner objektiven Identität willen einerseits die Rückkehr zum *Leben*; aber sie hat diese Form ihrer Unmittelbarkeit ebensosehr aufgehoben und den höchsten Gegensatz in sich. Der Begriff ist nicht nur *Seele*, sondern freier subjektiver Begriff, der für sich ist und daher die *Persönlichkeit* hat,—der praktische, an und für sich bestimmte, objektive Begriff, der als Person undurchdringliche, atome Subjektivität ist, der aber ebensosehr nicht ausschließende Einzelheit, sondern für sich *Allgemeinheit* und Erkennen ist und in seinem Anderen *seine eigene* Objektivität zum Gegenstande hat." ("The absolute Idea, as the rational Concept, that in its reality meets only with itself, is by virtue of this immediacy of its objective identity, on the one hand the return to *life*; but it has no less sublated this for its immediacy and contains within itself the highest degree of opposition. The Concept is not merely *soul* but free subjective Concept, that is for itself and therefore possesses *personality*—the practical, objective Concept determined in and for itself which, as person, is impenetrable atomic subjectivity, but explicitly *universality* and cognition, and in its other has *its own objectivity* for its object.").

21. *WdL. Die subj. Logik* (3. Abschn., 3. Kap.); *GW* 12: 253: "Das Übergehen ist also hier vielmehr so zu fassen, daß die Idee sich selbst *frei entläßt*, ihrer absolut sicher und in sich ruhend. Um dieser Freiheit willen ist die *Form ihrer Bestimmtheit* ebenso schlechthin frei,—die absolut für sich selbst ohne Subjektivität seiende *Äußerlichkeit des Raums und der Zeit*. Insofern diese nur nach der abstrakten Unmittelbarkeit des Seins ist und vom Bewußtsein gefaßt wird, ist sie als bloße Objektivität und äußerliches Leben; aber in der Idee bleibt sie an und für sich die Totalität des Begriffs und die Wissenschaft im Verhältnisse des göttlichen Erkennens zur Natur." ("The passage [from Concept to Nature] is therefore to be understood

here rather in this manner, that the Idea freely releases itself in its absolute self-assurance and inner poise. By reason of this freedom, the form of its determinateness is also utterly free—the externality of space and time existing absolutely on its own account without the moment of subjectivity. Insofar as this externality presents itself only in the abstract immediacy of being and is apprehended from the standpoint of consciousness, it exists as mere objectivity and external life; but in the Idea it remains essentially and actually [in and for itself] the totality of the Concept, and science in the relationship to nature of divine cognition.")

22. While it is true (as indicated in the following note) that it is above all in his Jena period that Hegel appears to entertain certain conceptions related to a certain rather somber romanticism, it is surely significant that in the second edition of the *Encyclopedia* (1827) Hegel would still dedicate a paragraph to the relation between "intelligence" and the "image": the latter, through being retained and in "interiorized" or "recollected" by the intelligence, ceases to be something unconscious that is stored or preserved in the depths of the soul. Hegel writes: "thus *recollected* [*erinnert*] within it [i.e., the intelligence], the image is no longer *preserved* as something which exists (unconsciously)" (§453; *GW* 19, 332). Hegel's "Note" to §453 goes on to develop this point, which is subsequently presented at greater length in the third edition (1830) of the *Encyclopedia* (See J. Derrida, "Le puits et la pyramide" in his *Marges de la philosophie*, Paris 1972, 79–127; *Margins of Philosophy*, translated by Alan Bass, Brighton 1982, 69–108). The first part of Hegel's "Note" from 1827 is retained in the third edition: "Die Intelligenz als diesen nächtlichen Schacht, in welchem eine Welt unendlich vieler Bilder und Vorstellungen aufbewahrt ist, ohne dass sie im Bewusstsein wären, zu fassen, ist dieselbe allgemeine Forderung überhaupt, den Begriff als concret [. . .] zu fassen" (*GW* 19, 332 ["To grasp intelligence as this night-like mine or pit in which is preserved a world of infinitely many images and representations, yet without being in consciousness, is the same as that general demand [. . .] that the Concept be grasped concretely"]. But in the 1830 edition Hegel also adds a decisive passage that allows us to recognize how hard he struggles to shake off the *primacy* of nocturnal associations here: "But intelligence as such is the free *existence* of *being-in-itself* which comes to collect or interiorize itself through its own development. Intelligence, therefore, must also be grasped as this *unconscious* mine or shaft, that is, as the existing *universal* in which nothing various has yet been posited in discrete terms" (*Enz.* §453, *Anmerkung*; *W.* 10, 260).

23. This conception of the "I" is developed by Hegel in the Jena period in particular, when he conceded a privileged significance to the

notion of the "night" that it is difficult to discover in precisely this form in his subsequent writings. Thus, in his early *Philosophy of Spirit* of 1805–6 (*Jenaer Systementwürfe III*) we read that for spirit "its primordial Self is object for it; the image, being as mine, as sublated [*aufgehoben*]." (One cannot fail to notice a certain similarity here to Lacan's idea of the "mirror stage"). The text continues as follows: "This image belongs to *it* [i.e., to spirit] [. . .] it is stored and preserved [*aufbewahrt*] in its hoard, in its night—it is *unconscious*, that is to say, without being brought out as object or presented before the power of representation. The human being is this night, this empty nothing, which harbors everything within its simplicity—a wealth of infinitely many representations and images, none of which currently occurs or presents itself to it—or which do not exist as something present. It is the night, the inwardness of nature, which exists here: *pure Self*" (*GW* 8, 186f.). In the *Phenomenology*, in the section of chapter VII dedicated to the "Light Essence," Hegel speaks of *self-consciousness* as confronted by actuality and says: "this is still only *its concept*, and this concept, in contrast with the daylight of this unfolding, is the night of its essence" (*GW* 9, 370; tr. Miller, 418). And in the final paragraph of the entire work, in a passage that is crucial for our interpretation here, Hegel speaks of spirit as follows: "As its fulfillment consists in perfectly knowing what *it is* [cf. the *to ti ēn einai* of Aristotle—F.D.], in *knowing* its substance, this knowing is its *withdrawal into itself* [*sein Insichgehen*] in which it abandons its outer existence [. . .] Thus absorbed in itself, it is sunk in the night of its self-consciousness" (*GW* 9, 433; Miller, 492).

24. *WdL. Die Lehre vom Sein* (1832). *GW* 21: 17f.

25. Compare, for example, Hegel's essay on *The Difference between Fichte's and Schelling's System of Philosophy* (*GW* 4, 17): "The manifoldness of being lies between two nights, without support. It rests on nothing" (Cerf and Harris, 95). See also the Jena *Philosophy of Nature* of 1805–6 (*Jenaer Systementwürfe III*, *GW* 8, 84: "The night harbours the self-dissolving process of fermentation and the disruptive struggle of all forces or powers [. . .] the tremor [*der Schauer*] of night is the quiescent life and stirring of all the forces or powers of substance; the brightness of day is their self-external being which has retained no inwardness, but is forfeited and spilled out as an actuality that is bereft of power and spirit."

26. *Enz.* §248, *Anmerkung*; *W.* 9, 28; *Hegel's Philosophy of Nature*, translated by Michael Petry, London 1970, vol. 1, 209. Petry translates *Abfall* here as "the Idea's *falling short* of itself."

27. *Enz.* §250, *Anmerkung*, *W.* 9, 35; Petry, vol. 1, 216: "the inability of nature to hold fast to the realization of the Notion [i.e. the Concept]."

28. Ibid., *W.* 9, 34; Petry, vol. 1, 215.

Notes to Chapter II

1. Saint Paul, *Letter to the Corinthians*, I, vv. 22–25 (cited from the Authorized Version).
2. *Kritik der reinen Vernunft*, B 131; tr. Kemp Smith, 152: "It must be possible for the 'I think' to accompany all my representations."
3. Novalis, *Hymnen an die Nacht*, V (*Werke*, edited by H.-D. Dahnke and R. Walbiner, Berlin/Weimar 1983, 10; Novalis, *Hymns to Night*, translated by Simon Elmer, Sorcerer's Apprentice 2011 (thesorcerersapprenticeonline. worldpress.com). The line is translated here as: "You are death, who at last makes us whole."
4. A. Emo, *Le voci delle muse*, Venice 1992, 41 (1965, 289).
5. *Enz.*, §475, *Zusatz*; *W.* 10, 298; see *Hegel's Philosophy of Mind, being Part Three of the Encyclopaedia of the Philosophical Sciences* (1830), translated by William Wallace and A. V. Miller, Oxford 1971, 237.
6. G. W. F. Hegel, *Vorlesungen über die Philosophie der Religion*, Teil I, edited by Walter Jaeschke, Hamburg 1983 (*Vorlesungen* 3, 10; abbreviated as *V-Rel.*, followed by the relevant volume number); *Lectures on the Philosophy of Religion*, 4 vols., translated by Peter Hodgson et al., Berkeley, CA 1984–97 (based on and including the pagination of the Walter Jaeschke edition), I, 10.
7. *Kritik der reinen Vernunft*, A 132 / B 171; Kemp Smith, 177.
8. The abstract concept, the concrete representation, and the community of the *cultus*, these are in effect the three moments in terms of which the "consummate religion" is presented and articulated by Hegel. This is very clear from the autograph manuscript of 1821, and with some variation of treatment in the lecture transcripts from 1824 and 1827.
9. See *Enz.* §248, *Anmerkung* (*W.* 9, 28); *Hegel's Philosophy of Nature*, translated by M. J. Petry, London 1970, vol. 1, 209. Petry translates *Abfall* here as "the Idea's falling short of itself."
10. *Enz.* §381 (*W.* 10, 17); *Hegel's Philosophy of Mind*, Wallace and Miller, 8.
11. *Wie wenn am Feiertage*, strophe 2, verse 4: "die mächtige, die göttlichschöne Natur" (Friedrich Hölderlin, *Werke und Briefe*, edited by F. Beissner and J. Schmidt, Frankfurt am Main 1969, vol. 1, 135; Friedrich Hölderlin, *Poems and Fragments*, translated by Michael Hamburger, London 1994, 395).
12. Ibid., strophe 1, verse 3: "wenn / Aus heisser Nacht die kühlende Blitze fielen" (*Werke und Briefe*, vol. I, 135; see also *Der Rhein*, strophe 13, verse 15: "Bevor das freundliche Licht / Hinuntergeht und die Nacht kommt" (*Werke und Briefe*, vol. 1, 152); *Poems and Fragments*, Hamburger, 442.

13. Wie wenn am Feiertage, strophe 3, verse 7: "wie einst, aus heiligen Chaos gezeugt" (*Werke und Briefe*, I, 135; *Poems and Fragments*, Hamburger, 394).

14. *Der Rhein*, the last verse (*Werke und Briefe*, I, 152; *Poems and Fragments*, Hamburger, 443).

15. *Friedensfeier* (the first version), strophe 5, verse 6 (*Werke und Briefe*, I, 158).

16. *Enz.* §377, *Zusatz* (*W.*10, 10; *Hegel's Philosophy of Mind*, Wallace and Miller, 1: "An out-and-out Other simply does not exist for mind").

17. *WdL. GW* 12,$_7$.

18. See *Phänomenologie des Geistes* (*GW* 9, 18, $_{4-5}$); Miller, 10.

19. *Enz.* §250, *Anmerkung* (*W.* 9, 35); *Hegel's Philosophy of Nature*, Petry, vol. 1, 215.

20. *WdL. GW* 12, 39, lines 18–20.

21. *WdL. GW 12*, 236, lines 17–18.

22. Many years ago, Mario Bunge entitled the first volume of his *Treatise on Basic Philosophy* as follows: *Ontology I: The Furniture of the World* (Dordrecht 1977). And only recently a collectively authored volume, written from an analytical perspective, came out with exactly the same name: *The Furniture of the World* (edited by G. Hurtado and O. Nudler, Amsterdam 2012).

23. *WdL. GW* 12, 39, lines 15–16.

24. See *Enz.* §246, *Zusatz* (*W.*9, 20) on the ceaseless character of these revolutions in the field of knowledge and of history (*Hegel's Philosophy of Nature*, Petry, vol. 1, 302: "All cultural change reduces itself to a difference of categories. All revolutions, whether in the sciences or world history, occur merely because spirit has changed its categories in order to understand and examine what belongs to it, in order to possess and grasp itself in a truer, deeper, more intimate and unified manner."

25. *WdL. GW* 12, 236, lines 14–15.

26. *Enz.* §247, *Zusatz* (*W.* 9, 25): "In der Natur verbirgt sich die Einheit des Begriffs"; *Hegel's Philosophy of Nature*, Petry, vol. I, 206: "In nature the unity of the Notion [that is, the concept] conceals itself." Incidentally, if we understand *Natur* (in a Spinozistic way) here as *natura naturata* (*ta physei onta*) and *Begriff* as *natura naturans* (*phusis-alētheia*), would this not lead us back to a reinterpretation of the famous fragment 123 by Heraclitus (*physis kryptesthai philei*)? This suspicion would be indirectly confirmed, in my view, by Hegel's praise of Schelling's reformulation of Spinoza's Substance: "Or the Spinozistic substance should not be understood as that which lacks movement, but as something manifesting intelligence [. . .] so that it is the *creative factor of nature*, but also, at the same time,

Wisdom and Knowledge." ("Oder die Spinozistische Substanz soll nicht als das Unbewegte, sondern als das Intelligente gefaßt werden [. . .]") *Vorlesungen über die Geschichte der Philosophie.* edited Michelet/Irrlitz-Gurst, Berlin 1984; III, 434 (my emphasis, F.D.).

27. Cf. *V-Rel.* 5, 176; Hodgson 3, 247.

28. *V-Rel.* 5, 270; Hodgson 3, 347: "The different positions are as follows: (a) immediate religion; (b) the Enlightenment of the understanding; (c) the rational cognition of religion."

29. *Enz.*§12, *Anmerkung* 1 (*W.* 8, 57); *Hegel's Logic, being Part One of the Encyclopaedia of the Philosophical Sciences* (1830), translated by William Wallace, Oxford 1975, 17: ("As a matter of fact, thinking is always the negation of what we have immediately before us). With as much truth however we may be said to owe eating to the means of nourishment, so long as we can have no eating without them. If we take this view, eating is certainly represented as ungrateful: it devours that to which it owes itself. Thinking, upon this view of its action, is equally ungrateful").

30. *Enz.* §471, *Anmerkung* (*W.* 10, 290); *Hegel's Philosophy of Mind*, Wallace and Miller, 230.

31. *Enz.* §74 (*W.* 10, 263); *Hegel's Logic*, Wallace, 108.

32. *Enz.* §554 (*W.* 10, 366); *Hegel's Philosophy of Mind*, Wallace and Miller, 292: "*Religion*, as this supreme sphere [that is, that of absolute mind or spirit] may be in general designated [. . .]"

33. *Philosophische Enzyklopädie für die Oberklasse*, §30 (*W.* 4, 66–68).

34. *V-Rel.* 5, 61; Hodgson 3, 126: "the moment of spirit in which it grasps itself inwardly, the moment of perishing to the natural."

35. *V-Rel.* 3, 104; Hodgson 1, 196: "[. . .] it is this negativity and movement of cutting off that constitutes my essence."

36. I have also explored this theme, drawing upon certain poetic suggestions in the work of Trakl and Celan, in my essay *La contrada dello straniero*, in *Aut Aut* 248–249, 1992, 63–74.

37. *V-Rel.* 5, 49 and 69; Hodgson 3, 115 and 133: "*Once is always.*"

Notes to Chapter III

1. George Lukács, *Der junge Hegel* (1948), Frankfurt 1973 (*The Young Hegel. Studies in the Relations between Dialectics and Economics*, translated by Rodney Livingstone, London 1975); Ernst Bloch, *Subjekt-Objekt. Erläuterungen zu Hegel*, Frankfurt 1962; Herbert Marcuse, *Reason and Revolution. Hegel and the Rise of Social Theory*, London 1955.

2. *Grosse Sowjet-Enzyklopädie* (Reihe: Länder der Erde), Berlin 1953, 278 and 282f.

3. G. W. F. Hegel, *Lectures on the Philosophy of World History. Introduction*, translated by H. B. Nisbet, Cambridge 1975, 195; this translation is based on the edition by Johannes Hoffmeister, *Philosophie der Weltgeschichte I. Vernunft in der Geschichte*, Hamburg 1980, 240. See also *Lectures on the Philosophy of History*, translated by John Sibree, London 1861, 106: "Lastly, the third part consists of the north-eastern States of Europe, Poland, Russia and the Slavonic Kingdoms. They come only late into the series of historical states, and form and perpetuate the connection with Asia." This translation was based on the edition by Karl Hegel (1840), which is reproduced in *Vorlesungen über die Weltgeschichte*, Suhrkamp 1970, *Werke*, vol. 12, 133.

4. We may recall Lenin's well-known response to Fernando de los Ríos when he asked him about freedom in the Soviet Union in 1920: "Yes, yes, the problem for us is not that of freedom, for with regard to that, the question we always ask is: freedom for what?" (*Mi viaje a la Rusia sovietista*, Madrid 1970, 37).

5. G. W. F. Hegel, *Grundlinien der Philosophie des Rechts* (= *Rechtsphil.*), *Vorrede*. edited by Gans/Klenner, Berlin 1981, 27; *Outlines of the Philosophy of Right*, translated by T. M. Knox, revised, edited, and introduced by Stephen Houlgate, Oxford 2008, 15: "Whatever happens, every individual is *a child of his time."*

6. See *On Revolution* (1963, London 1990. See also D. Barnouw, "Speech Regained: Hannah Arendt and the American Revolution," in *Clio* 15, no. 2 (1986), 137–52.

7. See my essay "Elogio de la frialdad. Sobre el Estado de la modernidad postrevolucionario," in *ISEGORIA* 10 (Madrid 1994), 167–78; see also my contribution: "Hegel: una época convulsa, entre la Revolución y la Restauración," in Las Actas del III Congreso Internacional: *La Filosofía y los retos de la complejidad*, La Sociedad Académica de Filosofía, Murcia 2006.

8. "Über die englische Reformbill," in *Berliner Schriften* (1818–31), edited by J. Hoffmeister, Neue Kritische Ausgabe, Hamburg 1956, XI, 506: "statt einer Reform eine Revolution herbeizuführen." *The English Reform Bill*, translated by T. M. Knox, in *Hegel's Political Writings*, edited by Z. A. Pelczynski, Oxford, 1964, 330. As a result of this electoral reform, in June 1832, the House of Commons opened its doors to representatives of the higher bourgeoisie, albeit not the petite bourgeoisie (let alone the proletariat).

9. Here I may be permitted to refer the reader to my study, *La Restauración—Las Escuela hegeliana y sus adversarios*, Madrid, 1999.

10. Karl Rosenkranz, *Hegel's Leben* (1844) (cited within in the text as Ros.), Wissenschaftliche Buchgsellschaft, Darmstadt 1977, 32. Rosenkranz is referring, of course, to the "Déclaration des Droits de l'Homme et du Citoyen" of 26 August 1789.

11. On this question, I would refer the reader to my essay. *Die Basis der europäischen Demokratie unter der Bedingung der Hegelschen "Verzeihung der Sünde,"* in R. Bubner and G. Hindrichs (eds.), *Von der Logik zur Sprache*, Stuttgarter Hegel-Kongress, 2005, Stuttgart, 2007, 549–63.

12. T. W. Adorno, "Skoteinos, or How to Read Hegel," in *Hegel. Three Studies*, translated by S. W. Nicholson, Cambridge, MA, 1993, 89.

13. We may remember Hegel's well-known remark from the Preface to the *Phenomenology of Spirit*: "Das Bekannte überhaupt ist darum, weil es *bekannt* ist, nicht erkannt"; *Phä. GW* 9, 26 (*Hegel's Phenomenology*, translated by A. V. Miller, Oxford 1970, 18: "Quite generally the familiar, just because it is familiar, is not cognitively understood"; cited in the text as: Miller).

14. The section of Hegel's text that we shall be discussing in some detail here is entitled "Absolute Freedom and Terror," part of chapter VI of the *Phenomenology of Spirit* (*GW* 9, 316–23; for this quotation, 320; Miller, 360, translation slightly adapted).

15. This explains, even if it does not exactly justify, why one recent Spanish translator of Hegel's text, M. Jiménez Redondo, has sometimes chosen to employ a whole range of different words and terms to render what is a single Hegelian expression (as well as accompanying his version with a host of elucidatory parentheses) in a desperate attempt to capture the multiple nuances embodied in the original terms and phrases.

16. To offer a rather more famous example: "Es kömmt nach meiner Ansicht, welche sich durch die Darstellung des Systems selbst rechtfertigen muss, alles darauf an, das Wahre nicht als *Substanz*, sondern ebensosehr als *Subjekt* auffzufassen und auszudrücken" (*Phä. GW* 9, 18). ("According to my way of looking at things, something which must be justified by the presentation of the system itself, everything depends on apprehending and expressing the True not as *Substance*, but just as much as *Subject* as well." (Miller, 9–10, on the other hand, writes, like the other older English translation by J. M. Baillie: "In my view, which can be justified only by the exposition of the system itself, everything turns on grasping and expressing the True, not only as *Substance*, but equally as *Subject*."). The original Spanish translator Wenceslao Roces (1966), like Jiménez Redondo later (2006), rendered this famous passage precisely and correctly, but it has been claimed that one should adapt the clause "nicht als Substanz" to include "sowohl" or "nur" so that the following comparison or elucidation

may make better sense (to read something like: "not so much—or not only—as Substance, but also as Subject"), thus implying that Hegel, either through haste or carelessness, had forgotten to indicate his meaning more precisely as required. As if, on the contrary, he were not rightly trying here—in a deliberately forced use of language—to bring out the "sublation" or "supercession" (*Aufhebung*) of Substance in and through the Subject, in which alone the former attains its highest *conceptual* significance.

17. I. Kant, *The Conflict of the Faculties* (Part 2: The Conflict of the Faculty of Philosophy and the Faculty of Law): "This revolution (Kant does not mention the French Revolution by name, but had referred few lines earlier to 'the revolution of a gifted [*geistreichen*] people'—F.D.) finds in the hearts of all spectators (who are not themselves engaged in this *Spiele* [the German word can signify both the activity of playing and a theatrical representation, like the English 'play'] a wishful participation that borders closely on enthusiasm the very expression of which is fraught with danger; this sympathy, therefore, can have no other cause than a moral predisposition in the human race" (Akademie-Ausgabe VII, 85; in I. Kant, *Religion and Rational Theology*, Cambridge 2008, translated by Allen Wood and George di Giovanni, 301–2). Rosenkranz alludes to the cultural and intellectual atmosphere, essentially sympathetic to the Revolution, that prevailed among the students at the Tübingen Stift, and remarks that "the bloody spectre of the Terror did not yet hinder enthusiasm for this *spectacle* [*die Hingebung an das Schauspiel*] of *seeing* a State coming into being on the basis of the Idea of the state, on the basis of the powers essential for its existence" (Ros., op. cit., p. 32; my emphasis).

18. In his *Biography*, Rosenkranz also includes a series of historic-political fragments that were probably composed by Hegel in his period in Bern (1795–98). Thus in one fragment that touches specifically on public executions, Hegel expresses his strong opposition to the practice, claiming that the spectacle of people dying at the hands of an executioner actually produces the opposite effect of that intended by judges and legislators, which was to produce "terror and fear [*Schrecken und Furcht*] at the thought of crimes." Hegel concludes that "the custom would result only in indifference [*Gleichgültigkeit*], as in the case of the warrior at whose right hand a thousand fall and at whose left hand ten thousand." And a little further on he compares those who perform the office of executioner as "blind instruments" of justice, with "the savage beasts to which criminals were once thrown" (Ros., 527; also in *W.* 1, 440–42; see also G. W. F. Hegel. *Fragments of Historical Studies*, translated by Clark Butler, in *Clio* 7, no. 1, 1977, 125).

19. In the *New Testament*, the word *katabolē* is always used in this sense of something collapsing, overturning, or coming to ruin (Mathew 13:35, 25:34; Luke 11:50, John 17:24; in the Pauline Epistles: Ephesians 1:4; Hebrews 4:3, 9:26, 11:11; also in Revelation 13:8 and 17:8; the corresponding verb *kataballō* appears at 2 Corinthians, 4:9; Hebrew 6:1; Revelation 12:10). However, here I am using the terms *katabolē* and *anabolē* more in the sense in which they are employed in modern biology: *catabolism* designates the disintegration of the products involved in cellular exchange, passing from complex molecules to simple molecules, liberating energy that is then exploited in the contrary process of *anabolism* to build up complex molecules. Catabolism is thus the body's appropriate reaction to a superabundance of energy, a reaction that in any case involves a certain destruction of the body's own substance. It seems that the proportional analogy between the process of biological *retro-alimentation* and the phenomenological process of the experience of consciousness works fairly well, except for the fact that in the case of molecular biology, the processes are alternating ones, whereas in Hegel's case the two phases are produced *simultaneously* (the ordinary consciousness that is observed suffers a *katabolē*—it collapses or finds itself ruined—while "we," the philosophical consciousness that observes, know that this is an *anabolē*—literally a turning upward in terms of the whole phenomenological path, or for the experience which Spirit undergoes in and through consciousness.

20. *Empirisme et subjectivité*. Paris, 2015; II: "La Raison se présente ici comme la conversation des propriétaires."

21. I have discussed this, from a different though parallel perspective (the step from Hume to Kant), in my book *De la libertad de la pasión a la pasión de la libertad*, Valencia, 1988.

22. *Phä. GW* 9, 321; Miller, 361 (translation slightly adapted): "The universal will, qua absolutely *positive*, actual self-consciousness, because it is this self-conscious reality which has *ascended* to the level of *pure* thought or of *abstract* matter changes round [*sich umschlägt*: is inverted] into its *negative* essence and shows itself to be equally that which *puts an end* [*Aufheben*] to the thinking of oneself, or to self-consciousness."

23. *Enz.* §112, Zusatz. W. 8, 233; *Encyclopedia of the Philosophical Sciences in Basic Outline, Part 1: Science of Logic*, translated by Klaus Brinkmann and Daniel O. Dahlstrom, Cambridge 2010, 175.

24. In the fifth paragraph of this work Descartes already confides that the publication of this account of his life "sera utile à quelques-uns," and in paragraph seven praises the science of mathematics for helping to "diminuer le travail des hommes" and also moral writings insofar as their

"exhortations à la vertu [. . .] sont fort utiles" (*Discours de la méthode*, Texte et Commentaire par É. Gilson, Paris 1947, 4 and 6; *The Philosophical Works of Descartes*, translated by E. S. Haldane and G. R. T. Ross, New York, NY 1955, vol. 1: *Discourse on Method*, 83 ("I hope that it will be of use to some without being hurtful to any") and 84 ("in Mathematics there are the subtlest discoveries and inventions which may accomplish much, both in satisfying the curious, and in furthering all the arts, and in diminishing man's labour; and that those writings that deal with Morals contain much that is instructive, and many exhortations to virtue which are most useful").

25. The celebrated apothegm that Kant famously chose as the motto for the *Critique of Pure Reason* may seem to contradict the Cartesian approach we have just mentioned (since there is no question here of recounting precisely how one has gone about one's life and one's studies—*de nobis ipsis silemus*—but rather of the task that is to be realized in common—*de re autem [. . .]*), but it fully concurs with Descartes as far as the ultimate end is concerned: it is ultimately a question of laying the foundations "utilitatis et amplitudinis humanae" (*Kritik der reinen Vernunft*, B II; the motto from Francis Bacon).

26. Whereas the word *Reich* (realm or empire) may signify a region, domain, or sphere of public power, *Land* (land or earth) implies by contrast the unmistakable sense of "country."

27. A world of unreality or one without actuality (*Wirklichkeit*) with respect to the previous world, the sensible and the supersensible world, for the new postrevolutionary consciousness corresponds to the idealism of the *understanding* that is merely subjective.

28. See *Phä. GW* 9, 433; Miller, 492: "Seine Grenze wissen, heisst sich aufzuopfern wissen" (Hegel is referring here to Spirit).

29. *Du Contrat social*; II, 3; *The Social Contract and Discourses*, translated by G. D. H. Cole, London 1973, 185.

30. Louis Antoine Léon (de) Saint Just, *Discours et rapports*, edited by Messidor, Paris 1988, 171.

31. This can be observed in the so-called "Bolivian Revolution" of Venezuela today. Thus Hugo Chávez could declare: "I wish and I ask that we leave this ideological Congress as a single political party, the great historical party of the Bolivian revolution." In effect, and thereby repeating the gesture of Saint Just (in a rather Borgesian way, it has to be said), Chávez thinks that the existence of various parties only threatens to sow divisions. What is needed, therefore, is a "great mechanism" that could transcend the usual electoral parameters: "I do not know what name it will bear, but it will be the only party, a single party that must represent the Republic before

the world" (see Pedro Pablo Peñaloza, "Chávez desea partido único," in EL UNIVERSAL.com, Caracas, 10 September 2006). Now of course we do know the name: it is called *Chavism*. Or what amounts to the same thing: the identification of the universal with an individual, with a singular self. And this was already perfectly expressed in a kind of premonition by Antonio Paso, A. Dominguez, and F. Chueca in the "zarzuela" *El bateo* (*Tango de Wamba*): "WAMBA: The way we are now, / If things go on like this, / the fire and dynamite / will surely come // The way they treat us / in the end we'll cry: Up with the socialists and down . . . / Chorus: What? / WAMBA: That is not allowed to say. / But the day I get to govern, / if I ever get to govern, / ten thousand heads at least / will have to roll. // Of human flesh we'll build / a statue of Robespier [*sic*] / to allow that martyr / to serve as an example. / We'll make two hundred parts / of all the nation's gold. / One for all of you, and the rest . . . / Chorus: What? / WAMBA: . . . for this humble servant of you."

32. *Die fröhliche Wissenschaft*, 3. Buch, §125, KSA 3, 481: "Ist nicht die Grösse dieser That zu gross für uns? Müssen wir nicht selber zu Göttern warden, um nur ihrer würdig zu erscheinen?"; see Walter Kaufmann, *The Portable Nietzsche*, New York 1970, 96: "Is not the greatness of this deed too great for us? Must not we ourselves become gods simply to seem worthy of it?"

33. Information and quotation derived from the article "Guillotine" in *Wikipedia*.

34. *WdL*. Book I, section 1a, chapter 3, B.c; *GW* 11, 155f.

35. Moreover, Hegel expressly links the higher specific gravity with the "absolute Lord" from the phenomenological context: with Death, clearly identified in turn with *l'Être suprème* or *das höchste Wesen*—the *essence* that both internally devours every being and simultaneously allows it to live. See *Hegel's Philosophy of Nature*, Petry, vol. II, 157f.: "The high specific gravity is precisely an *undisclosed being-in-self*, a simplicity which has not yet been broken up [. . .] and is also, therefore, a lack of form as particularization or specification" (*Enz.* §320, *Zusatz; W.* 9, 265; my emphasis).

36. We are dealing here with a spectacular, and expressly speculative, inversion of the "particularization" of the individual in the *Philosophy of Right* (*Rechtsphil.* §52, *Anm., W.* 7, 166; *Outlines*, 66: "Owing to the qualitative differences between natural objects, mastery and occupancy of these has an infinite variety of meanings and involves a restriction and contingency that is just as infinite. Apart from that, a generic 'kind' of thing, or an element as such, is not the correlative object of an individual person. Before it can become such and be appropriated, it must first be individualized into a

breath of air or a drink of water [*ein Schluck Wassers*])." The expression I have emphasized here is clearly the same as that employed in the *Phenomenology* with regard to death in the context of the revolution. But the sense here, just as evidently, is the inverse one: in the *Philosophy of Right* I begin to be a personal singular being when I assimilate what is external: the air that I breathe, the water that I drink, cease to be something generic *in actu exercito*. Playing on, and extending, the words of Descartes, we could then say: *nego naturam, ergo sum* (ultimately thought itself is already a negation of what is natural, external, and immediate, as we know from the opening chapter of the *Phenomenology*). Nonetheless, this very ingestion may be the cause of death, that is, can ensure that the singular person returns to the elemental and the generic. In our case this death is intentionally brought about by another singular being that—in a striking confirmation of what we have already seen in the struggle to the death between different self-consciousnesses—believes that it can dominate the other when it converts the latter into the Other per se, into what is *dead*.

37. *Briefe von und an Hegel*. Hamburg, 1952, I, 12; G. W. F. Hegel, *The Letters*, translated by Clark Butler and Christiane Seiler, Bloomington, IN 1984, 29.

38. A good number of articles on this sinister figure are easily accessible on Google.

39. Compare the *Manifest der Kommunistischen Partei* (1848), Stuttgart 1969, 27: "Alles Ständlische und Stehende [in the political sphere—F.D.] verdampft, alles Heilige [in the supersensible world of faith—F.D.] wird entweiht, und die Menschen sind endlich gezwungen, ihre Lebensstellung [. . .] mit nüchternen Augen anzusehen"; the *Manifesto of the Communist Party*, in Karl Marx and Friedrich Engels, *Selected Works*, London 1968, 38: "All that is solid melts into air, all that is holy is profaned, and man is at last compelled to behold with sober eyes his real position in life, and his relations with his kind" (translation slightly adapted). This last phrase reveals the full distance that separates Marx from Hegel: for the former, the Enlightenment—and its consequences, the Revolution—have proved to be a "cleansing process," a means of delivery—albeit a violent one—from the strange relics of the past, a kind of preparation that compels human beings—or will compel them, by means of a further and definitive revolution—to behold their position in life with "sober eyes." For Hegel, on the other hand, the Revolution has dissolved every "position in life." And it is only by interiorizing this event in a moral, Kantian, and post-Christian consciousness, in the domain of "conscience," that this *absolute negativity* can be acknowledged or confronted. We could thus put it this way: Marx

rather conceals—or implicitly justifies—the subjective horror produced by the objective Terror, just as Kant had already attempted to "comprehend" the violence involved through its theatrical metamorphosis into an *edifying spectacle*: edifying, on a general level, in view of the progress it represents on the part of the human race or *kind* (*Gattung*), not in view of the individuals who suffer the Terror or those who conceptualized it rather than employing it precisely as an example.

40. *Phä. GW* 9, 316; Miller, 355: *Beyde Welten sind versöhnt, und der Himmel auf die Erde herunter verpflanzt*.

41. *Briefe*. 1, 24; *The Letters*, Butler, 35–36.

42. This is Hyperion's objection to the revolutionary figure of Bellarmin in Letter 7 of Hölderlin's novel (*Sämtliche Werke und Briefe*, Darmstadt 1998, vol. 1, 636).

43. Here we are irresistibly reminded, by way of specific comparison and explication, of the words with which Hegel considers the triumph of *la Nation une et invisible* and "elevates it to the concept" in 1806: "Diese ungetheilte Substanz der absoluten Freyheit erhaebt sich auf den Thron der Welt, ohne dass irgend eine Macht ihr Widerstand zu leisten vermöchte" (*Phä. GW* 9, 317; Miller, 357: "This undivided Substance of absolute freedom ascends the throne of the world without any power being able to resist it.")

44. See *La Révolution française. La Terreur* (3), available at: diagnopsy.com/Revolution/Rev-061.htm.

45. *Phä. GW* 9, 27: "die ungeheure Macht des Negativen." Here, in the Preface to the *Phenomenology*, as is well known, Hegel expressly compares the power of "the understanding" (*Verstand*) with death, describing the latter, this supposed unreality (which is in truth *die reine Wirklichkeit*) as "the absolute power" (*die absolute Macht*) (Miller, 19). That is why the interiorization of death, the process in which each consciousness becomes aware of the *volonté générale* and the incarnation of the latter in *la Nation*, will correspond precisely to absolute freedom.

46. *Vorlesungen über die Geschichte der Philosophie*, *W.* 20, 297. It is not exactly a mark of intellectual probity that Joachim Ritter, in his essay on *Hegel und die französische Revolution* (in his collection: *Metaphysik und Politik*, Frankfurt am Main 1969, 196), cites this text as an example of Hegel's admiration for the *Aufklärung* and for the revolution that ensued, but also cuts the quotation off precisely here, "forgetting" that in what immediately follows after a full stop, and not even in the next paragraph, Hegel adds the remarks that I have just quoted in the main text above.

47. *Philosophy of History*, 466. We should observe how what was offered in 1806 as a fact (or, more precisely, as a result of the phenomenological

experience of the particular "shape" or *Gestalt* of Enlightenment), namely the reconciliation between the world of truth, or Heaven, and actual reality, the Earth (*Phä. GW* 9, 316; Miller, 355), is presented here in a more distanced way (this is what was thought *then*) and in terms of a subjunctive *als ob* (it was *as if* we had arrived at this reconciliation, which implies that in fact or in the event, *in der Tat*, this was not actually so).

48. *Enz. W.* 8, 12ff.; Brinkmann and Dahlstrom, 6 (from the Preface to the first edition—1816—of the *Encyclopaedia*; my emphasis).

49. In a letter addressed to the president of the Royal Society in London (of 20 March 1800) and subsequently published in the *Philosophical Transactions* of the Society. It was also in the early 1800s that Nicholson and Carlisle succeeded in breaking down water into hydrogen and oxygen (present in all processes of combustion and for that reason—according to the reflections of Hegel, and not only of Hegel—intimately connected with fire.) Precisely by interpreting the result of this experiment in reverse, it was thought at the time that fire, when extinguished—with the separation of the oxygen (*Sauerstoff*)—released free hydrogen (*Wasserstoff*: "the stuff of water"). In any case, it is hardly possible for us today to appreciate the enthusiasm and fascination that the galvanic pile produced on all sides and the effects that it exercised in the electrochemical context, from Kant's *Opus posthumum*, where he almost identified his philosophy with galvanism, to Mary Shelley's *Frankenstein*. This was not so surprising since this was the first time that scientists had discovered a source capable of generating a continuous current of energy in significant quantities. In his *Notice biographique* of 1831, Dominique François Arago lauded the galvanic pile in the following terms: "And indeed, I have no doubt in saying that this seemingly inert mass, this strange mixture, this pile of different metals separated by a little liquid, is, in terms of its singular effects, the most marvelous instrument that has ever been invented by man, including the telescope and the steam engine" (cited in A. Aldaz Riera, *Electroquímica y pilas de combustible: de antaño a hogaño*, Discurso inaugural en la Facultad de Ciencias de la Università de Alicante, 1991).

50. *Enz.* §283, *Zusatz*; *Hegel's Philosophy of Nature*, Petry, vol. II, 39 (translation adapted). Here we should remember the One (*das Eins der Individualität*) over against the many ones that were excluded and repelled from it; see chapter III, note 34 above.

51. It almost seems as if there were some powerful subterranean current connecting this Jena text with *La ginestra, o il fiore del deserto* (*The Broom, or the Flower of the Desert*), the famous poem in which Leopardi celebrates the efforts of enlightened man in his struggle with Nature: "ed

ordinate in pria l'umana compagnia, / tutti fra sé confederati estima gli uomini, / e tutti abbraccia con vero amor" ("and thinking the company of men to be conjoined at first, / He [the enlightened man] considers all confederate amongst themselves, / and embraces all with unfeigned love"). Certainly, in both cases the final result is a tragic one: Nature ultimately prevails over the deeds and desires of human beings. But whereas the poet laments *la condition humaine* in melancholy terms, the Jena Hegel, still very much influenced by Greek tragedy, seems to recognize the *hybris* of man and his fatal destiny in trying to exceed his limits.

52. Ros., 180; see G. W. F. Hegel, *The System of Ethical Life and First Philosophy of Spirit*, translated by H. S. Harris and T. M. Knox, New York, NY 1979, 255.

53. See my essay "La difícil doma de Proteo," in *Hegel. Especulación de la indigencia*, Barcelona, 1990.

54. *Zum ewigen Frieden*, Article 2, Akadamieausgabe, VIII, 356; *Toward Perpetual Peace*, translated and edited by Mary J. Gregor, in I. Kant, *Practical Philosophy*, Cambridge 1996, 327.

55. J. J. Rousseau, *Du Contrat social*; II, 3: "J'appelle République tout Etat régi par des lois."

56. *Rechtsphil.* §4; *W.* 7, 46; *Outlines*, Knox, 26.

57. *Metaphysics*, I, II: 982b 25ff.

58. *Jubiläumsausgabe*, ed. H. Glockner, Stuttgart 1958, VI, 396; *Hegel's Political Writings*, Knox, 282.

59. Ibid., VI, 395; *Hegel's Political Writings*, Knox, 281.

60. See chapter III, note 13, above.

61. *Hegel desde Adorno. En torno a "Tres Estudios sobre Hegel,"* in CRISIS XVIII/70–71 (1971) 142–50; cit., 142.

62. Antonio Machado, "Proverbios y cantares" LXXXV, *Nuevas canciones*. Madrid, 1924.

Notes to Chapter IV

1. Cf. *WdL. GW* 12: 253 lines 22 and 29: Di Giovanni, 752–53, where *sich entläßt* is also translated as "discharges itself."

2. *De duabus naturis*, c. 3; ed. Migne, P.L. 64, 1343: "persona est rationalis naturae individua substantia." Hegel will obviously substitute *substantia* for *Subjekt*, which, nonetheless, does not entail a remarkable change, for in the scholastic tradition *substantia* can be understood as *hypostasis humanae naturae*. (compare Thomas Aquinas, *Summa contra Gentiles* c. 4, 38).

3. Thomas Aquinas, *Summa Theologiae*. I, 29, a. 3 ad 4. *m*. The person is *individuum*: "secundum quod important incommunicabilitatem." And more precisely (in I, 29; q. 4. *Resp*.:) "Individuum autem est quod est in se indistinctum, ab aliis vero distinctum." The person is *relativa* (*ib*.:) "Persona igitur divina significat relationem ut subsistentem." And therefore the person is *substantia* (I. 29, a. 3 ad 4. m.): "secundum quod significat existere *per se*" (my emphasis).

4. Boethius, *De duabus naturis*, c. 3. P. L. 64, 1344: "Nomen personae videtur traductum ex his personis quae in comoediis tragoediisque homines repraesentabant [. . . .] Graeci vero has personas 'prosopa' vocant, ab eo quod ponientur in facie, atque ante oculos obtegant vultum."

5. *Rechtsphil*. §62, *Anm*., 95 s. and <u>Anhang</u> ad loc. n. 8: 432; Knox, 74.

6. Th. Veblen, *The Theory of the Leisure Class*. (Cited in L. Dickey, *Hegel*. Cambridge/New York 1987, 250).

7. Saint Paul, *Galatians* 4, v. 4.

8. *V-Rel*. 5, 95; Hodgson 3, 161: "that spells an end."

9. *Phä. GW* 9, 362_{25}; Miller, 409: *das versöhnende JA*.

Notes to Chapter V

1. Mark 3: 28–9. The Authorized Version has "the Holy Ghost" here for "the Holy Spirit."

2. *Philosophie der Natur, Enz*. §248, *Anm*., *W*. 9, 28: "So ist die Natur auch als der Abfall der Idee von sich selbst ausgesprochen worden, indem die Idee als diese Gestalt der Äusserlichkeit in der Unangemessenheit ihrer selbst mit sich ist." See *Hegel's Philosophy of Nature*, translated by M. J. Petry, London 1970, vol. II, 209: "nature has also been regarded as the Idea's *falling short* of itself, for in this external shape the Idea is inadequate to itself." In his translation of *Hegel's Philosophy of Nature* (Oxford 1970), A. V. Miller translates "*der Abfall der Idee von sich selbst*" as "the self-degradation of the Idea."

3. *V-Rel*. 5, 77; Hodgson 3, 141.

4. F. Creuzer, *Sileno,* edited by F. Duque, Barcelona 1991, 74.

5. *WdL. GW* 12, 187, lines 34–35; Di Giovanni, 684; see also earlier in the text, 146: "to feel pain is the privilege of sentient nature."

6. *WdL, GW* 12, 166, lines 23–24; Di Giovanni, 663: "purpose—as the concept that concretely exists freely over against the object and its process."

7. (*V-Rel*. 5, 45; Hodgson 3, 109; the whole passage reads as follows in Hodgson's translation: "By consciousness of the unity of divine

and human nature we mean that humanity implicitly bears within itself the *divine idea*, not bearing it within itself like something from somewhere else but as its own substantial nature, 'as its own vocation or the unique possibility of such a vocation: this infinite possibility is its [i.e., humanity's] subjectivity.'").

8. *Enz.* §24, *Zusatz* 3; *W.* 8, 89; *Encyclopedia of the Philosophical Sciences in Basic Outline, Part I: The Science of Logic*, translated by Klaus Brinkmann and Daniel O. Dahlstrom, Cambridge 2010, 64: "In fact the act of entering into opposition, i.e. the awakening of consciousness, is intrinsic to human beings themselves; it is a history that repeats itself with every human being."

9. Saint Paul, *I Corinthians*, 3, v. 16.

10. Saint Paul, *I Corinthians* 15, v. 20; the Authorized Version reads: "But now is Christ risen from the dead, and become the first fruits of them that slept."

11. *V-Rel.* 5, 153; Hodgson 3, 222: "Hence the sensible representation includes the coming again of Christ, which is essentially an absolute return, but then takes the turn from externality to the inner realm—a Comforter who can come only when sensible history in its immediacy has passed by."

12. *Propädeutik* (*W.* 4, 68); *The Philosophical Propaedeutic*, translated by A. V. Miller, Oxford 1986, 169.

13. *Enz.* §376, *Zusatz*: "Das Ziel der Natur ist, sich selbst zu töten" (*W.* 9, 538); *Hegel's Philosophy of Nature*, Petry, vol. III, 212: "The purpose of nature is to extinguish itself." Miller translates the sentence as: "The goal of nature is to destroy itself" (*Hegel's Philosophy of Nature*, 444).

14. From *phasis*, as the inexpressible root of all *kataphasis* and *anaphasis* (cf. *Metaphysics*, XII, 1072b, 15ff.).

15. This is how the triad appears in Hegel's autograph manuscript of 1821:Hodgson 3.133–62. It is true that in the lecture transcripts for 1824 and 1827 the third term is replaced, not without a certain loss of logical clarity, by the *Realisierung des Glaubens* or the *Realisierung des Geistigen der Gemeinde*. But fundamentally the scheme remains intact inasmuch as this "realisation" is accomplished in philosophy rather than in the religious community, which, as such, *has passed*, or rather *continues to be always past.*

16. *V-Rel.* 5, 267; Hodgson 3, 345: "This is the standpoint of philosophy, according to which the content takes refuge in the concept and attains its justification by thinking."

17. Preface to the 1827 edition of the *Encyclopaedia* (*W.* 8, 23f.); Dahlstrom I, 15 (translation adapted).

18. *V-Rel.* 5, 91; Hodgson 3, 155. In this connection Ricardo Ferrara, the Argentinian translator of these lectures, actually points out that "Calvin, in contrast to Zwingli, does not reduce the Eucharistic presence of Christ

to a mere memorial [. . .], but teaches instead the virtual presence of the glorified body of Christ."

19. Mathew 5, v. 13.

20. Saint Paul, *Letter to the Galatians*, 4, v. 4.

21. (*V-Rel.* 5, 95; Hodgson 3, 160: "When [religious truth is] treated as historical, that spells an end [to it]."

22. In the so-called "Fortsetzung des Systems der Sittlichkeit" (J. Hoffmeister, *Dokumente zu Hegels Entwicklung*, Stuttgart 1936, 314–25, specifically 323); the "Conclusion of the System of Ethical Life," as Rosenkranz called it, is included in: Hegel, *System of Ethical Life and First Philosophy of Spirit*, translated by H. S. Harris and T. M. Knox, New York, NY 1978, 178–86; see 185.

23. Harris and Knox, 185.

24. Harris and Knox, 324.

25. *V-Rel.* 5, 269; Hodgson 3, 347—see *Philippians* 4, v. 7 (in Luther's version: *der Friede Gottes, welcher höher ist als alle Vernunft*).

26. G. W. F. Hegel, *Vorlesungen über die Philosophie der Geschichte*, Band 1, *Die Vernunft in der Geschichte*, ed. by J. Hoffmeister, Hamburg 1994, 34–35; Hegel, *Lectures on the Philosophy of World History. Introduction*, translated by H. B. Nisbet, Cambridge 1980, 32.

Index

Abfall (waste), ix, 26, 36, 94, 116
Absolute, the, viii, ix, 25, 27, 51, 88
Absolute Lord, the, 43, 44, 67, 69, 97, 99, 101
activity, 9, 10, 19, 20, 32
 continual, 13
 of spirit, 37
 of thinking, 9, 21
actuality, 26, 79, 88, 101
Adam, 45
adequation, 19
Adorno, Theodor Wiesengrund, 62, 91
Alles Übrige (Everything else), 94
anabolē, 66
Ancien Régime, 59, 84, 91
Antigone (Sophocles), 115
appearance, 21, 22–24, 44, 52, 65, 68, 125
Arendt, Hannah, 58
Aristotle, vii, 1, 3–6, 8–16, 86, 92, 127
Asia, 57

Bacon, Francis, 69
beautiful soul, 84
becoming, 1, 11, 89

being, viii, ix, 1, 2, 4, 5, 7–11, 22, 23, 25, 38, 39, 68, 70, 88, 89, 94, 98, 117, 120, 122
being-for-another, 79, 98
being-for-itself, 96, 98, 99, 103
being-for-self, 74, 79
Berlin, 32, 44, 59
Berlin Wall, 58
Beyond, the, 95–98, 102, 120, 121
Boethius, 98
bourgeois, the, x, 89, 91
bread and wine, 36, 37
Büchner, Georg, 77

cabbage, head of, 62, 63, 71, 75
Calvinism, 123, 129, 131
Carlsbad Decrees, the, 59
Carrier, Jean-Baptiste, 76, 77, 79
categorematic/noncategorematic, 62
categories, 9, 23, 98
Catholic thought and doctrine, 30, 48, 49, 110, 122, 128, 129, 131, 133
cause, 2
 formal, 4
 immanent, 41
 material, 4

157

Celan, Paul, 77
chemical process, 82
chemical transformation, 75
chora, 37, 48
Christ, 30, 35, 36, 44–46, 49–53, 110, 111, 115, 120, 123
Christianity, 30, 31, 32, 35, 36, 44, 102, 118, 133
citizen, 49, 72, 88–90
civil society, 90, 122
Clauberg, Johannes, 7
closure, ix, 13
Code Civile, 85
common sense, 62
community, x, 35, 36, 41, 47, 49, 53, 54, 60, 66, 90, 91, 98, 123
  Christian, 102, 110
  of the faithful, 35, 36, 54, 109, 120
  of philosophy, 40
  subterranean, 22, 84
concept, ix, 19, 22–27, 33, 34, 36, 38, 40, 45, 49, 60, 78, 82, 90, 93, 94, 96, 102, 118, 123, 125, 134
conciliation, 22
consciousness, 15, 16, 19, 20, 21, 34, 42, 43, 52, 54, 65, 66, 69, 86, 119
  individual, 85
  lordly and servile, 67
  religious, 40
constant presence, 1
Constitution, the, 87, 89, 90, 91
contradiction, 31, 97, 101
Convention Nationale, 76, 77, 80
Correggio, Antonio di Pellegrino di Allegri, 45
Cratylus, 1
crime, 71, 72, 90, 104, 109

Cross, the, 31, 48, 50–53, 66
culture, 36, 37
cultus, 35, 36, 124, 126

De anima (Aristotle), 16
de Chirico, Giorgio, 73
death, 11, 31, 32, 36, 37, 46–48, 50–54, 56, 62, 63, 64, 65, 66, 67, 69, 70, 71, 74, 75, 80, 81, 83, 88, 97–99, 115–117, 119, 120, 134
  of Christ, x, 29, 31, 35, 50, 52, 132
  of death, 48–50, 52, 53, 113
Déclaration des droits, 70
definition, 5, 9, 11, 14
deject, 26, 27
Deleuze, Gilles, 67
delusion (*Wahn*), 14
Descartes, René, 7, 14, 15, 16, 69
Desmoulins, Camille, 77, 80
destiny, 41, 94, 95
determinateness, 89, 122
determination, 4, 6, 8, 11, 12, 23, 27, 49, 94–96, 101, 102, 122
development, 22, 23, 25, 33, 34, 124
Devil, the, 2, 116, 117, 120
Dickens, Charles, 64
dialectic of master and slave, 99
dialectical materialism, 56
difference, 95, 100, 101
disenchantment of the world, 122
divine nature, the, 118, 121
doctrine of essence (Hegel), 88
doctrine of objectivity (Hegel), 22, 26
doctrine of subjectivity (Hegel), 22
dwelling, 32, 42

earth, 36, 38, 45, 53, 91
eidos, 5, 6, 7, 12, 13, 20
Einmal ist allemal (once is always), 51, 98, 120, 134
element
 of freedom, 88
 liquid, 75
 logical, 26
 negative, 85
Emmaus, 48
Emo, Andrea, 31
emptiness, 30
Encyclopaedia of the Philosophical Sciences (Hegel), 35, 41, 56, 82, 90, 96, 102, 106, 108, 125, 126
end, 10, 11, 32, 118
end of time, 53, 133
Enlightenment, 40, 41, 59, 69, 70, 79, 80, 82, 86
ens rationis, 61
epochē, 52
Ereignis (the event), 52
essence, 4, 6, 9, 11, 22–25, 41, 78, 88–90, 99, 101, 124, 125
 common, 99, 100
 concrete, 122
 negative, 68, 75
essentialities, 21, 39
estate, 40, 41, 42, 85, 87, 89, 109
eternity, 47, 53
ethics, 14
Être supreme, 69, 73
Europe, 60, 69
 Southern, 55
European Union, 55
existence, 10, 11, 22, 24, 25, 32, 45, 49, 51, 52, 89, 102, 103, 118, 133
experience, 65, 67, 69, 90

exposition, 95, 125
exteriority, 39, 96, 101
externality, 88, 89, 95, 99, 100
externalization, 22, 117

factions, formation of, 72, 78
facts, 60, 61, 65, 91, 131
 of consciousness, 14
faith, 33, 40, 45, 51, 53, 70, 105, 110, 111, 127, 129, 130, 132
faithful, the, 53, 54, 109, 110, 131
family, the, 44, 49, 90, 123
fanaticism, 80
Father, the, 35, 36, 45, 47, 49, 53, 120, 121
Faust (Goethe), 17
feeling, 42, 119
Fichte, Johann Gottlieb, 14, 19, 24, 41, 56, 75, 79
Fideism, 41
finitude and the finite, 51, 103, 119, 125, 126, 132
fire, 80, 81, 82, 89, 91, 120
flesh and blood, 36
forgiveness of sins, 6, 133
form, 16, 20, 23, 42
foundation, 15, 30, 34, 35, 53, 102, 124
France, 65, 70, 76, 84, 87, 89, 90
Frederick the Great, 8
Freedom, 15, 35, 49, 50, 58, 67, 77, 80, 86, 88, 91, 98, 100–103, 121, 122, 133
 absolute, x, 64, 65, 68–71, 75, 76, 83, 86, 89
 negative, 76
 revolutionary, 65
French Revolution, the, 55, 56, 58, 59, 61, 64, 65, 86, 91, 102
fundamentum, 15, 16, 18

fury of destruction (in *Phenomenology of Spirit*), 73, 86
Fürwahrhalten, 65

Gadamer, Hans-Georg, vii
Gaea, 36
galvanic pile, 81
Gemeinde (the spiritual community), 36, 44, 60, 90, 91, 102, 109, 123, 124
Gemeinschaft (the community), 90, 91, 103
genesis, 23, 24
German Idealism, viii, 56
Germany, 60, 70
God, x, 9, 10, 11, 13, 15, 27, 30, 32, 33, 34, 35, 36, 37, 44–48, 53, 60, 73, 96–98, 101, 109, 111, 112, 115, 116, 117–119, 121, 123–127, 129, 131–133
  Bacchic, 40
  God-Man, the, 36
  Hebrew conception of, 35
Goethe, Johann Wolfgang von, 17
Gorgias, 1
Greece, 15, 29, 30
ground, 1–3, 15, 16, 37, 51, 52, 93, 121, 123
guillotine, 71, 73–75

head, 41, 48, 61, 71–75, 77, 87, 92
heaven, 38, 53, 91
Heidegger, Martin, 1, 3, 13, 64, 95
Heraclitus, 25, 62
Herod, 35
hermeneutics, viii, 34
history, 14, 34, 44, 51, 52, 117, 121, 133
Hölderlin, Friedrich, 37, 62, 79

Holy Roman Empire of the German Nation, 87
Homer, 8
human being, 2, 9, 13, 29, 32, 35, 36, 41, 42, 43, 44, 45, 46, 50, 51, 53, 72, 73, 77, 79, 86, 97, 102, 105, 115, 116, 118, 119, 120, 122, 123, 124, 126, 128, 132
human
  nature, 118, 121
  subject, 15
humanity, 57, 60
hylé, 3, 7, 16, 37
hyparchei, 6, 7, 8
Hyperion (Hölderlin), 79
hypokeimenon, 1, 3, 6–13, 15, 16, 20

I, the, 15, 16, 19, 24, 26, 27, 29, 31, 32, 43, 73, 79, 81, 122
I = I, 20
  night of the, 26
  subjective, 20
Ich bin der Kampf selbst (I am the very struggle), 29
Idea, the (Hegel), viii, ix, x, 23, 25, 26, 34, 36, 38, 39, 51, 93–97, 99, 102, 116, 118, 121
identity, 42, 88, 89, 98
Ignatius of Loyola, 52
Iliad, 8
Imitatio Christi, 46
immortality, 9, 46
impotence, 9, 27, 38
in der Tat (in fact), 66, 68
incarnation, 35, 50
individual, the, 9, 10, 11, 18, 32, 49, 53, 60, 85, 90, 91, 99, 100–102

Index

individuality, 24, 71
industrial capitalism, x
infinitude, 51, 103, 106, 111, 119, 125, 131
inherence, 11–13
inhesion, 22
innocence, 117, 120
intellection, 9, 10
intuition, 9, 41

Jacobi, Friedrich Heinrich, 14, 41, 95
Jahweh, 30
Jena, 83, 85
Jerusalem, 3
Jesus, 35, 36, 45, 47, 48, 53, 116, 120
Joachim da Fiore, 98, 133
José I, 60
Judea, 120
Judgment, 6, 9, 12, 90
 apodictic, 45
 identical, 20
 of necessity, 90
 negative infinite, 78, 90, 115
July Revolution, the, 59

Kant, Immanuel, vii, 14, 18, 19, 35, 55, 64, 65, 67, 68, 70, 78, 79, 85, 91
katabolē, 66, 69
Kingdom
 of God on Earth, 98
 of Heaven, 48
 of Spirit, 40
knowing, 27, 42, 98, 117, 134
Kojève, Alexandre, 63

Lagerkvist, Pär, 60

language, 5, 26
law, 18, 45, 70, 89, 102, 122, 124
Lessing, Gotthold Ephraim, 98
liberty, equality, and fraternity, 65
life, 10, 11, 27, 31, 36, 44, 49, 51, 54, 93, 94, 97, 99, 117, 118, 121, 133, 134
 divine, 13
 ethical, 36, 44, 49, 91, 100, 121–123, 133
 natural, 50
 negative, 75
 perfect, 10
 of the spirit, 66
 supreme, 10
limit, the, 51, 98
liquefaction, 78
logic, ix, 7, 8, 21, 26, 32, 94, 95
 of inhesion, 35
 objective, 22
 subjective, 22, 25, 26
 subsumption, 35
 unconscious, ix, 26
logic of being (Hegel), 22
logic of the Concept (Hegel), 124
logic of essence (Hegel), 22, 24, 26
logical element, the, 35, 94, 117
logos, ix, 4–7, 9, 11, 12, 37, 40, 53, 124
Lord, the, 43, 44, 97, 99, 100, 101, 108, 119
Louis, Antoine, 74
Louis XVI, 73, 74
Lukács, Georg, 56
Luke, Saint, 47
Luther, Martin, 49, 52, 53, 120, 124

man, x, 44–46, 119, 121

Marcuse, Herbert, 56
Mark, Saint, 117
Marx, Karl, 55
Mary Magdalene, 45–48
Master, the, 85, 99
matter, 2–4, 7, 8, 9, 12, 16, 20, 84, 97, 99, 100, 125, 133
  basic matter (*die Sache*), 21
  logical, 16
mediation, 26, 35, 36, 122
Mephistopheles, 17
Messiah, 48
metal, 74
Metaphysics (Aristotle), 3, 4, 8–10, 12, 126
metaphysics, vii, x, xiii, xiv, 1, 2, 7–9, 11, 13, 14, 21, 32, 42
method, vii
  acroamatic, vii
  dialectical, viii, 55
  dialectical-speculative, x
  hermeneutic, vii, viii
Midas, 117
middle term (*Mitte*), 25, 46, 71, 91
modern subjectivism, 15
modernity, 13, 15, 69
  syllogism of, 70
moment, 34, 66, 101, 107, 108
  logical, 36
monarch, the, 7, 8, 107
Montesquieu, Charles de Sécondat, 69
moral conscience, 70
moral enthusiasm, 64
morality, x, 60, 79, 119
morphē, 6, 12
mortality, 46
mythology of reason, 29

nachdenken, 21, 26

name, 4, 5
Nantes, 76, 80, 82
Napoleon Bonaparte, 60, 65, 84, 85, 87
narrative symbolism, 71
la Nation, x, 69, 81, 88–90
nature, ix, x, 9, 10, 21, 22, 26, 27, 35, 36, 37–40, 45, 47, 49, 50, 51, 70, 81, 83–85, 96, 99–103, 105, 106, 108, 109, 116, 118
necessity, 88, 91
  absolute, 88, 90
  logical, 96
needs, 103, 105, 132
  system of, 104–106, 111
negation, 96, 100, 103
  abstract, 73, 115, 116
  determinate, 53, 94, 102
  dialectical, 33
  double, 53, 99
  infinite, 96
negativity, 25, 68, 88, 98
neo-empiricism, 61
New Testament, 48
night, 26, 27, 37
Nietzsche, Friedrich, 73
noēsis noēseōs, 10
non-I, 24, 100
nothing, 89, 116
nous, 16
Novalis, Friedrich von Hardenberg, 31
les noyades, 77, 80
Nuremberg, 44, 88

object, 10, 20, 21, 23, 26, 70, 99, 118
objectivity, 91, 94, 96
objectum, 11
  intelligible, 10

October Revolution, 57
omnimode determinatum, 94
omnitudo negationum, 96
One, the, 10, 13, 85, 97, 101
  Governing One, the, 75
  the One and the many 'ones,' 74, 76
  One of individuality, the, 75
  logical, 75
  singular, 75
  supreme, the, 11
ontic and logical dimension, 6
onto-politological argument, 78
ontotheology, 13
ontology, 7
opinion, 18
origin, 10, 11, 26, 45, 118
other, the, and otherness, 17, 22, 23, 25, 27, 30, 38, 39, 66, 93, 95, 98–99, 121
ousia, 5, 6, 8, 9, 11
oxidization and reduction, 82

pain, 117, 118
pantheon, 35
Paraclete, the, 53, 120, 121
Parmenides, 1
particular, the, 73, 90
particularity, 24, 35, 36, 89, 120, 121
passion, 50, 67, 120, 133
Paul, Saint, 30, 45, 47, 48, 66, 133
peace, 133
Pelagius, 98
Pentecost, 53
people, the, 72, 75, 76, 122, 124, 133
person, x, 93–103
personality, 93, 94, 98, 102, 122
Phaedo (Plato), 31, 98

phasis, 12
Phenomenology of Spirit (Hegel), viii, 17, 20, 23, 24, 33, 37, 38, 55, 60, 62, 67, 71, 83, 84, 86, 101
Philosophical Propaedeutic (Hegel), 44
philosophy, 12, 32, 40, 42, 59, 60
  ancient, 8, 14
Philosophy of Nature (Hegel), ix, 74, 81, 83
Philosophy of Religion (Hegel), 32, 40, 117, 118
Philosophy of Right (Hegel), 90
phusis, vii, 10, 25
Plato, 32, 52, 83, 98
point of indifference, 22
Poland, 57
Politische Theologie (Carl Schmitt), 123
Pontius Pilate, 35
positing, 93
possibility, 57, 79, 108, 115, 118, 119
power, 30, 38, 101, 116
  of the negative, 80
praxis, x, 43, 66
predicate and predication, 6, 8, 9, 11, 12, 94
praeparatio mortis, 32, 98
presence, 13, 38
principle, 3, 4, 8–11, 14, 18, 23
prima philosophia, vii
Primo de Rivera, José Antonio, 118
prior inscription, 11
process, 34, 43, 102
  dialectical, 123
production, 70
progress, 32
Proofs of the Existence of God (Hegel), 41

property, 4, 11, 102, 103
proposition, 14
  speculative, 120
protē ousia, 9, 16
Protestantism, 44, 133
Proverbs, 69
Prussia, 56, 64
Psyche, 52

Quevedo, Francisco De, 51, 52

Ranke, Leopold von, 33
rationality, 61, 90
realitas objectiva, 16
reality, 23, 25, 60, 97, 100
reason, 39, 40, 41, 95, 133
  speculative, 39
  sufficient, 39
  universal, 60
Reason and Revolution (Marcuse), 55
reconciliation, 60, 66, 81, 117, 119, 121
Redeemer, the, 36, 45, 120
redemption, 49, 120, 121
reflection, 3, 19, 21, 40, 41, 52, 89, 91, 100, 122, 124
  absolute, 24
  double, 22
reflexive circularity, 4
Reform Bill, 59
Reinhold, Karl Leonhart, 14
relation, 20, 21, 93, 98, 99
  of inner and outer, 77
  of substantiality, 24
relation-to-self, 20
relationality, 14, 25, 98
religion, 29, 32–37, 40–44, 49, 52, 66, 91, 96, 121–124, 133, 134
remains and the remainder, ix, 12, 26, 27, 38, 51

Renan, Ernest, 95
representation, 26, 36, 42, 125
republic, 85, 87
res publica, 99, 100
Restoration, the, 59, 89, 91
resurrection, 44, 51, 120
return to life, the, 25
revolution, x, 58, 59, 64, 65, 73, 74, 77, 79, 81, 82, 84, 87
right, 60, 87, 88, 100, 102
Robespierrre, Maximilien de, 76, 77, 79, 80
Rome, 35, 64, 99, 102
rootlessness, 29
Rosenkranz, Karl, 44, 60, 83
Rousseau, Jean-Jacques, 67, 68, 70, 71, 85
ruin and ruination, 66, 133, 134
Russia, 57

Sache (basic thing or matter), ix, 2, 18, 21, 97
sacrifice, 35, 49, 50, 115, 119–121
Saint-Just, Louis Antoine de, 72, 76
salvation, 31
Schelling, Friedrich Wilhelm Joseph, 56, 59, 64, 76, 79
Schmitt, Carl, 123
Schopenhauer, Arthur, 31
Science of Logic (Hegel), viii, ix, 25, 26, 33, 45, 62, 88, 93
second nature, 47, 49, 70, 104
secularization, 122
self and selfhood, 22, 27, 88, 100, 101, 116, 121
self-abnegation, 50
self-affirmation, 25
self-annihilation, 32
self-certainty, 99

self-consciousness, 20, 34, 43, 67, 68, 69, 71, 79, 86, 90, 99–101, 119, 124
self-determination, 34, 49, 122
self-emptying, 35
self-knowing, 25
self-negation, 20
self-positing, 20
self-reference and self-referential unity, 17, 22–24, 89
self-sameness, 24
series of contraries, 9
Sieyès, Emmanuel-Joseph, 85
Silenus, 117
simple, 9, 12, 13
simple relation to itself, 23
singular, 68, 90
singularity, 35, 36, 45, 49, 77, 100, 115, 121, 122
Sittlichkeit (ethical life), 47, 50
skepsis, 1
Slavic world, 56, 57
slave, the, 99, 101
society, 41, 44, 53, 102, 122–124
 industrial, x
 market-governed, x
socialism
 real existing, 58
 scientific, 56
Socrates, 31
Son, the, 35, 48, 118, 121
Soul, 17, 32, 43, 52
Soviet orthodoxy, 55
Soviet Union, 58
Spain, 60, 90
species, 5, 6, 7, 10
spectacle, 64
specter (*revenant*), 78
speculative geopolitics, 70
Spinoza, Baruch, 13, 14, 23, 27

spirit, ix, x, 9, 21, 26, 27, 34–39, 42, 44, 45, 46, 60, 66, 116, 117, 119, 120, 124, 133
 absolute, 42, 91, 96, 101
 finite, 26, 45, 116
 Holy, 48, 49
 objective, 50, 91
 self-conscious, 70
 subjective, 40
spiritual masses, 65, 69
Stalin, Joseph, 56
Ständeschrift (Hegel), 87
state, the, x, 8, 30, 44, 49, 69, 70, 78, 85, 86, 89–91, 122–124
structure, 14
struggle, 43, 72, 83, 134
 for recognition, 67
subject, the, x, 2, 3, 5–27, 35, 38, 40, 67, 93, 99, 101–103, 124
 of attribution, 12
 free subject, 15
 in general, 11
 individual, 18, 19
 finite/infinite, 20
 predication, 15
 primary, 11
 thinking, 21
 transcendental, 19
Subjekte, 7
subjectivity, 29, 87, 91, 94, 118
 atomic, 25, 94, 95
 free, 34
 impenetrable, 95
 of reflection, 14
subjectum, 11
sublation, 22, 33, 53, 66, 98
substance, x, 4–6, 17, 23–26, 35, 69, 71, 85, 89, 101, 124
 absolute, 19, 124

substance *(continued)*
  abstract, 1, 3, 4, 8, 9, 11, 17, 18, 21, 22, 2
  ethical, 86, 90, 101, 123, 124
  individual, 12, 16, 99
  inner, 71
  primary, 5, 6, 7, 9, 12, 13, 22, 24
  secondary, 5, 7, 9, 12, 13, 16, 22, 24
substantial nature, 118
substantiality, 90, 99, 100
  indifferent, 74
substrate, 3, 4, 8, 9, 11, 12, 17, 18, 21–25, 103
subsumption, 11
sujet proposé, 2
supernaturalism, 30
Supreme Being, the, 81, 101
syllogism, 3
system, x, 17, 23, 74, 86

Tathandlung (Fichte), 68
tautology, 6
terminus medius, 45, 70
Terror, the, 58, 59, 61, 62, 63, 64, 65, 67, 70, 71, 73, 76–79, 82–92
that which is *(to on)*, 1
theoria, x, 43
theos, 13
Thermidore, 75, 84
thing, 1, 2, 4, 6, 10, 11, 18, 19, 21, 26, 29, 97, 102, 103
  external, 24
  in general, 24
  itself, 4, 18, 100
  natural, 45
thought, 10, 16, 21, 25, 26, 32, 33, 59, 93, 96, 134
  abstract, 36, 42, 80
  objective, 21
  speculative, 52

time, 9, 14, 34, 35, 37, 47, 52, 53, 59, 60, 118, 120
  fulfilled, 35
to ti ēn einai, 7, 13
tode ti, 6, 11, 15
totality, 35, 99, 120
Towards Perpetual Peace (Kant), 85
Tractatus de intellectus emendatione (Spinoza), 27
transcendental leap, 16
transition, 89
True, the *(das Wahre)*, 17, 19–21, 23, 24, 95
Truth, viii, ix, 4, 6, 7, 14, 15, 19, 21, 22, 24, 26, 27, 30, 31, 34, 36, 42, 47, 51, 57, 65, 69, 70, 79, 89, 92–94, 99, 101, 109, 111, 112, 118, 119, 123–125, 127, 128, 130–132, 134

Umschlag (reversal), 68, 69, 80, 82, 83, 89, 90
understanding, the, 41, 62, 80, 89
universal, 68, 71, 72, 73, 90
  abstract, 81
  concrete, 91
universality, 21, 24, 35, 42, 45, 49, 88, 99, 100, 121, 122
universal history *(Weltgeschichte)*, 51, 57, 81, 87, 133
universe, 10
Untertan (political subject), 7
utility, 103

Verbum, 30, 53, 132
Virgil, 52
vita activa, 93
vita contemplativa, 70, 93
volonté générale, 67
Volta, Alessandro, 81

war, 85
 civil, 66
water, 71, 76, 81, 82, 83, 84
water, gulp of, 62, 63, 71, 75, 92
West, the, xi
the what it is to be (*to ti ēn einai*), 4
whole, the, 23, 24, 26, 95
 concrete, 17
 in Hegel, 22
 organic, 17
will, the, 67, 117
 general, 71, 78, 89
 individual, 89
 singular, 71, 78, 91
 of the universal, 91
Wirklichkeit (effective reality), 26, 45, 69

wisdom, 29, 30, 41
Wohlfahrt, Günther, 61
word, 5, 8, 10, 30, 49, 95, 97, 124
 of God, 119
 of the Rite, 36
world, 21, 23, 26, 50, 78, 81, 86, 90, 96, 122, 133
 external, 21, 45
 Greek, 35, 101
 modern, 102
 real, 41
 sensible, 68, 70, 82
 supersensible, 68, 70
World Spirit, 57, 60, 86
Württemberg, 87

Zeno of Elea, 1
zoē, 10

www.ingramcontent.com/pod-product-compliance
Lightning Source LLC
Chambersburg PA
CBHW021143230426
43667CB00005B/232